T0362745

Social Studies
SKILLS
Book 2

A WORKBOOK FOR HOMEWORK AND REVISION

RUTH NAUMANN

NELSON
A Cengage Company

Australia • Brazil • Japan • Korea • Mexico • Singapore • Spain • United Kingdom • United States

Social Studies Skills Book 2
1st Edition
 Ruth Naumann

Cover designer: Cheryl Rowe
Text designer: Cheryl Rowe
Production controller: Siew Han Ong
Reprint: Natalie Orr

Any URLs contained in this publication were checked for currency during the production process. Note, however, that the publisher cannot vouch for the ongoing currency of URLs.

Acknowledgements
Acknowledgements
The author and publisher wish to thank the following for photographs:
Shutterstock, cover and pages4, 5, 8, 9, 11, 12, 13, 14, 16, 18, 23, 27, 29, 31, 32, 36, 37, 42, 44, 45, 49, 50, 51, 55, 58, 71. Humanrights.net for logo on page 19. Tremain, Garrick, ATL for cartoon on page 60. Hawkey, Allan Charles, ATL for cartoon on page 61.

© 2012 Cengage Learning Australia Pty Limited

For product information and technology assistance,
in Australia call **1300 790 853**;
in New Zealand call **0800 449 725**

For permission to use material from this text or product, please email
aust.permissions@cengage.com

National Library of New Zealand Cataloguing-in-Publication Data
National Library of New Zealand Cataloguing-in-Publication Data

Naumann, Ruth.
Social studies skills : workbook for homework and revision / Ruth Naumann. (New Zealand basics)
ISBN 978-017023-076-6 (bk.1)—ISBN 978-017023-077-3 (bk.2)
1. Social sciences—Problems, exercises, etc.—Juvenile literature. [1. Social sciences—Problems, exercises, etc.] I. Title. II. Series.
300.76—dc 23

Cengage Learning Australia
Level 7, 80 Dorcas Street
South Melbourne, Victoria Australia 3205

Cengage Learning New Zealand
Unit 4B Rosedale Office Park
331 Rosedale Road, Albany, North Shore 0632, NZ

For learning solutions, visit **cengage.com.au**

Printed in Singapore by C.O.S. Printers Pte Ltd.
10 11 12 13 14 15 25 24 23 22 21

Contents

ISBN: 978-0170-23-077-3

1 Understanding documents

Think about identity, culture and organisation: how groups make decisions that impact on communities, and how people define and seek human rights.

A document is any form that is used to communicate facts, information, decisions or comments. The most translated document in the world is **The Universal Declaration of Human Rights**.

| belonging and applying to everyone in the world without exception | a document of things that countries agree upon but which are not legally binding | person, about people | freedoms to which people are entitled |

- It was adopted by member countries of the United Nations, including New Zealand, in 1948 at a gathering at a palace in Paris.
- It is reasonably short. You can download the whole document in about three pages.
- It consists of a Preamble (introduction to a document saying why it was created and what it aims to do) and 30 Articles (sections in a document).
- Each Article sets out a right. For example, Article 3 says all humans have the right to life, liberty and security. Article 4 says slavery and the slave trade are banned. Article 23 says everyone has the right to work, to free choice of employment, to just and favourable conditions of work, to protection against unemployment, to equal pay for equal work, to fair pay, to join trade unions.

Practice 1

Decide which image you would choose to put on the cover of your research project about The Universal Declaration of Human Rights. State your decision and the reasons for it in the space below.

Image 1

Skill: Decision-making

- This asks you to select from two alternatives. Think of criteria you could use such as colour, emotional reaction, message, interest value.
- Think of **pros** (for) and **cons** (against) for each. Writing them on a separate sheet of paper will help you see things more clearly.
- You can weight your pros and cons by giving them a mark out of 5. For example '*I feel uncomfortable seeing a person in a cage (5)*' in the con column means you feel strongly about that, whereas '*The globe stands for world-wide (1)*' in the pro column means you don't rate that as vitally important. Add up the points in each column.
- If you don't like the answer this process gives you it means you haven't included all the pros and cons or you haven't scored them consistently.

ISBN: 978-017023-077-3

Practice 2

Read the introduction to this unit again, especially what Article 23 says, and explain how the following images are related to human rights.

Skill: Relating
- This asks you to explain what specific items (images) have to do with a general concept (human rights).
- Ask yourself questions such as, 'Is the existence of a trade union likely to be considered a basic human right?'

"If you really wanted the job, you'd be willing to do it for nothing."

ISBN: 978-017023-077-3

2 Interpreting official documents

Think about culture, identity and organisation: how people define human rights.

Practice 1

The left side of the chart below is a simplified version of the **Universal Declaration of Human Rights**. The right side is an explanation for the articles. Match them up by putting article numbers after the explanations.

Skill: Integrating
- This involves connecting or combining information. For example, Article 1 is a general statement about freedom and equality at birth for all, so look for an explanation that addresses that.
- Look for key matching words. For example, Article 29 is about duties so what word from the explanations might match that word?

1 Everybody is born free and equal.	Asking another country to protect you.
2 No discrimination.	Asking for legal help to get human rights.
3 The right to life.	Asking for help against harm to your name.
4 No slavery.	Attending school.
5 No torture.	Belonging to a country.
6 You have rights no matter where you go.	Following or changing your beliefs.
7 Everybody is equal before the law.	Freedom to choose a job and get paid for it.
8 Your human rights are protected by law.	Getting rest and holidays.
9 No unfair detainment.	Having legal protection everywhere.
10 The right to trial.	Keeping your possessions.
11 Innocent until proven guilty.	Living in freedom and safety.
12 The right to privacy.	Marrying who and when you want.
13 Freedom to move.	No punishment for something you didn't do.
14 The right to seek a safe place to live.	No society or group can destroy rights.
15 The right to a nationality.	No unjust imprisonment.
16 The right to marriage and family.	Not being subjected to cruel treatment.
17 The right to your own things.	Organise and attend peaceful meetings.
18 Freedom of religion.	Public trials, not secret ones.
19 Freedom of expression.	Responsibilites.
20 The right to public assembly.	Sharing your community's arts and sciences.
21 The right to democracy.	Skin colour and gender make no difference.
22 The right to social security.	Slavery and the slave trade are not allowed.
23 Everybody has workers' rights.	Social and international order.
24 The right to play.	Taking part in your country's politics.
25 Food and shelter for all.	Law applies in the same way to everyone.
26 The right to education.	Think and say what you like.
27 The rights to culture and copyright.	Travelling within and outside your country.
28 A fair and free world.	Universal freedom and equality at birth.
29 Everyone has duties to the community.	Whatever you need to survive.
30 No one can take away your rights.	Your society helps you develop.

ISBN: 978-0170-23-077-3

Practice 2

Study the 10 articles below which are from the Declaration. Match them to the simplified version in Practice 1 by putting their numbers after them. Then highlight 20 words you would add to a glossary to go with the Declaration.

Skill: Integrating
- This involves studying legal and official language. Look for key words as clues; for example, born, opinion, law.
- Note that the articles talk of 'him' and 'his'. They are inclusive terms that stand for females as well.
- Remember; **glossary** here would mean a list of legal and official words.

Nothing in this Declaration may be interpreted as implying for any State, group or person any right to engage in any activity or to perform any act aimed at the destruction of any of the rights and freedoms set forth herein.

Everyone, as a member of society, has the right to social security and is entitled to realisation, through national effort and international co-operation and in accordance with the organisation and resources of each State, of the economic, social and cultural rights indispensable for his dignity and the free development of his personality.

Everyone has the right to freedom of opinion and expression; this right includes freedom to hold opinions without interference and to seek, receive and impart information and ideas through any media and regardless of frontiers.

Everyone has the right to freedom of thought, conscience and religion; this right includes freedom to change his religion or belief, and freedom, either alone or in community with others and in public or private, to manifest his religion or belief in teaching, practice, worship and observance.

No one shall be subjected to arbitrary interference with his privacy, family, home or correspondence, nor to attacks upon his honour and reputation. Everyone has the right to the protection of the law against such interference or attacks.

Everyone is entitled in full equality to a fair and public hearing by an independent and impartial tribunal, in the determination of his rights and obligations and of any criminal charge against him.

Everyone has the right to an effective remedy by the competent national tribunals for acts violating the fundamental rights granted him by the constitution or by law.

All human beings are born free and equal in dignity and rights. They are endowed with reason and conscience and should act towards one another in a spirit of brotherhood.

All are equal before the law and are entitled without any discrimination to equal protection of the law. All are entitled to equal protection against any discrimination in violation of this Declaration and against any incitement to such discrimination.

Everyone is entitled to all the rights and freedoms set forth in this Declaration, without distinction of any kind, such as race, colour, sex, language, religion, political or other opinion, national or social origin, property, birth or other status. Furthermore, no distinction shall be made on the basis of the political, jurisdictional or international status of the country or territory to which a person belongs, whether it be independent, trust, non-self-governing or under any other limitation of sovereignty.

ISBN: 978-017023-077-3

3 Interpreting images

Think about culture, identity and organisation: how people define and seek human rights.

Practice 1

Write a sentence for each image in the collage below to show how it is related to the idea of human rights.

> **Skill: Expressing ideas clearly**
> - You have only one sentence so you need to make sure you write your ideas as accurately as you can.
> - Consider each image separately. It might show a positive aspect such as people taking part in a political debate, a right not everyone in the world has. It might show a negative aspect such as slavery which is still present in the world today.

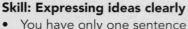

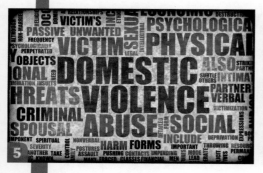

1 _____

2 _____

3 _____

4 _____

5 _____

6 _____

7 _____

8 _____

ISBN: 978-0170-23-077-3

Practice 2

Use the images below to help you list ways people work to get human rights.

> **Skill: Inferring**
> - This means going beyond available information to identify what could reasonably be true. For example, if peaceful group protests are shown, could you expect people to protest as individuals, and to use violent protests also?
> - Always read questions properly; 'to help you' means you don't have to restrict your answer to what the images show.

Located at Guantanamo Bay in Cuba, Guantanamo is a US detention and interrogation centre for prisoners such as those captured in wars in Afghanistan and Iraq. Some are said to be Muslim extremists who have dedicated their lives to killing Americans and are considered too dangerous to be freed. Abuse of some prisoners has caused international controversy.

The July 1 protest is an annual event in Hong Kong, originally led by a Human Rights group after the handover of Hong Kong from Britain to China in 1997. It is a time for people to voice their wish for human rights.

The Headquarters of the United Nations is located in New York city in the US. It includes the General Assembly where member countries meet; each of the 192 delegations has six seats, three at a desk and three behind them. There are three other regional headquarters. One is at Geneva in Switzerland and houses the Human Rights Council. Promoting and protecting human rights has been a major aim of the United Nations. The United Nations' Human Rights Day is annually observed December 10 to mark the anniversary of the presentation of the Universal Declaration of Human Rights.

The United Nations Peace Palace is in a city called The Hague in the Netherlands. It houses the International Court of Justice which settles legal arguments brought to it by countries. Also in The Hague is the International Criminal Court which prosecutes individuals for things such as crimes against humanity and war crimes.

Clever posters are a way of alerting people to human rights abuses.

_____
_____
_____
_____
_____
_____
_____

ISBN: 978-017023-077-3

Recognising violations

Think about culture, identity and organisation: how people define and seek human rights.

A violation, sometimes called an abuse, is an act that disregards a right such as a human right defined by the Universal Declaration of Human Rights, or an agreement such as a treaty. The Crown, for example, can be said to be in violation of the Treaty of Waitangi if it has confiscated land from Maori who fought against the British and Government during the 1860 wars in New Zealand because today's understanding is that Maori took up arms to save their land.

Practice 1

The 16 terms below in the bottom box are from the Declaration of Human Rights where it addresses violations. Put the terms with their meanings.

Skill: Applying terms to definitions
- Some of the definitions are very similar so you need to study them closely to find points of difference.
- Always do the easier ones first.
- Use what you already know. For example, think of the difference between a slave and a servant and you will understand slavery and servitude.

having no respect for someone or something	action of inflicting severe pain on someone as punishment or coercion	causing a loss of self-respect
cruel and unjust government or rule	unjust and cruel treatment that goes on for a long time	savagely cruel
being barred from your country, often for political reasons	ignore	unfair behaviour towards a person or group because of a factor such as race, age, gender, religion
	people owned by someone	
getting, transporting and selling people as slaves	continual cruel treatment of a person or group because of a factor such as race, age, gender, religion, beliefs	bound to an owner or master for a particular time
acts of unusual or illegal cruelty	determined by personal choice or whim rather than a fair or legal system	lacking kindness or compassion

• arbitrary • atrocities • barbarous	• contempt • degrading	• discrimination • disregard • exile	• inhuman • oppression	• persecution • servitude • slavery	• torture • tyranny • slave trade

ISBN: 978-017023-077-3

Study each violation of human rights below and verify, preferably by internet research, if it is true or false. Write **T** or **F** after it with a note of explanation.

Skill: Verifying
- This means confirming the accuracy of something. Here you are given a guide as to what to use for this – the net.
- Choose a key word to search under. It should be specific. Some are obvious, such as Recife; some will need more thought.

Saudi Arabia bans millions of girls from taking part in PE classes in school and denies many females access to facilities such as gyms, sports clubs, and swimming pools.

In the city of Recife, known as Brazil's murder city, death squads which include police officers have carried out so many summary executions of 'killables' such as street children, that a group has put up an electronic body counter in the middle of the city.

The effort by leader Pol Pot in the 1970s to form a communist peasant society in Cambodia through forcing urban dwellers to relocate to the countryside to work on collective farms and forced labour projects, combined with executions, killed an estimated 1.7 to 2.5 million people out of a population of about 8 million, and is an example of genocide.

The abduction of children and either trafficking them out of their country to work or forcing them into the military as child soldiers, sex slaves, spies, messengers, lookouts, and porters occurs in many countries.

Honour killings, where members of a family or social group murder another member because of perceived shame the member has brought, happen to more females than males.

The Disappeared are people whom a state or political group abducts, imprisons, tortures, kills and buries in a secret place, and then refuses to discuss the people's fate or location.

There are more slaves today than were seized from Africa in four centuries of slave trading.

ISBN: 978-0-17023-077-3

Recognising discrimination

Think about culture, identity and organisation: how people define and seek human rights.

Discrimination is a common human rights violation. In New Zealand you have the right to freedom from discrimination on the grounds of sex, marital status, religious belief, ethical belief, colour, race, ethnic or national origins, disability, age, political opinion, employment status, family status, and sexual orientation.

Practice 1

Study the resources below and comment on how each one is showing actual or possible discrimination.

Skill: Recognising discriminatory practices and behaviour
- This is about values which influence the ways people think and act, and whether people's values cause them to treat someone differently to how they treat others.
- Ask yourself if anyone is being treated differently or unfairly on any of the grounds given for New Zealand.

Resource 1 A 60-year-old gets a job on a building site. The foreman introduces him as Joe but all the other workers keep calling him other names such as Grandpa, Fossil, and Geriatric.

Resource 2

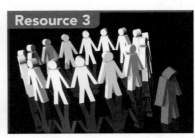
Resource 3

Resource 4

"We're all terribly excited you are joining the club."

Resource 5

"Alright, now fire everyone who's right-handed."

Resource 6 Travelling on a bus, as the only passenger, is a girl with learning disabilities. The driver stops at an ATM and when he gets back the girl asks if she is on the right bus. She takes a while to ask because of her disability. The driver gets impatient and verbally abuses her.

1 _____
2 _____
3 _____
4 _____
5 _____
6 _____

ISBN: 978-017023-077-3

Practice 2

Study the table and photo below. Explain why you could not use them as evidence of discrimination without explanations, and comment on what the explanations should talk about

Government	2001	2011
Maori Public Sector	17.0%	16.4%
Maori Senior Managers	9.7%	9.2%
Pacific Island Public Sector	6.6%	7.6%
Pacific Island Senior Managers	1.8%	1.6%
Asian Public Sector	3.4%	7.4%
Asian Senior Managers	1.7%	1.9%

Source: NZ State Services Commission

Skill: Assessing
- This practice asks you to estimate the quality and value of a resource.
- Firstly check for a source. For example, as the table comes from the NZ State Services Commission, the data will be accurate.
- Check what else you would need to know before using the table as evidence of discrimination. For example, would it help to know that Maori at that time comprised 15 percent of the population and Asians 9 percent?

_____

_____

_____

_____

_____

_____

_____

_____

_____

_____

_____

ISBN: 978-017023-077-3

Understanding group decisions and impacts

Think about identity, culture and organisation: how groups make decisions that impact on communities, and how people define and seek human rights.

Practice 1

Read the following and highlight actions and beliefs that showed discrimination of Jews.

Skill: Recognising discriminatory practices and behaviour

- This is a values exploration skill; you need to think about how the Nazi government discriminated against Jews.
- Look for ways the Jews were treated differently to others; for example, did Aryans have to wear identification signs that showed they were Aryans?

Jude is German for Jew.

A group of people in Germany voted Adolf Hitler into power in the 1930s and later allowed him to become Führer (leader) in whose hands all political power rested. Hitler led the National Socialist German Workers' Party (Nationalsozialistische Deutsche Arbeiterpartei or Nazis). This group dominated Nazi Germany, also called The Third Reich (Reich is empire and there had been two previous empires). Through groups such as the Gestapo (secret state police) and the SS (Schutzstaffel, armed wing of the Nazi Party) the Nazis got rid of political opposition, took away the human rights of millions of people, and led Germany into World War 11 (1939-45). Nazis talked of a group of white Germanic people, which they called Aryans, as the master race and a group of sub-human inferiors such as Jews, gypsies, Poles, Russians, and Hungarians. They blamed Jews as a group for Germany's problems and banned them from professional jobs such as doctors and teachers. Government contracts could not go to Jewish businesses. The SS carried out the Night of Broken Glass when they smashed windows of Jewish shops and offices, and destroyed Jewish synagogues and homes. Jews were forced to close their businesses and shops and sell them for a fraction of their worth. Aryan doctors could treat only Aryan patients. Jewish children were not allowed to go to state schools. Jews were not allowed to marry non-Jews and Jews became 'subjects of the state' rather than citizens, which meant they no longer had rights such as the right to vote. Signs saying 'No Jews' were posted outside towns, restaurants, shops. Jews had to hand in their gold and silver objects and their jewels; their radios were confiscated. Jews with non-Jewish first names had to add Israel to their names if they were male or Sara if they were females. A large J had to be printed on their passports and they had to wear the yellow Star of David, a sign of Judaism. They were subject to a curfew and moved into ghettos, densely-packed Jewish suburbs, inside cities. The Final Solution was the planned extermination of Jews from Europe and the holocaust refers to the killing of about six million Jews in concentration camps.

ISBN: 978-017023-077-3

Practice 2

Read the following and highlight with three different colours the definitions of human rights violations used at Nuremberg, examples of the definitions, results of Nuremberg. Then in the blank box put your opinion about whether the Nuremberg trials should have been held or not.

Skill: Exploring values
- Since values are the beliefs and ideas shared by a group about what is desirable and good and what is not, putting people and groups on trial means their actions are being measured against what is believed to be desirable and good.
- When giving your opinion consider the actions from your viewpoint and ask questions such as, 'Did the Allies have the right to put Nazis on trial'?

During and after the war against Nazi Germany, the four major allied powers - US, UK, France, Soviet Union - talked about Nazi violations of human rights. They decided to define these human rights violations and create a court called the International Military Tribunal to try individuals and groups. This resulted in the Nuremberg trials, held in the city of Nuremberg in Germany 1945-46 at the Palais of Justice, which was spacious, largely undamaged by bombing, had a big prison, and was where the Nazis had held annual propaganda rallies. The Nuremberg trials were to prosecute only captured high-ranking Nazi officials and groups such as the Gestapo and the SS. Several Nazis such as Hitler committed suicide before the trials began. The definitions used were war crimes, crimes against humanity, and crimes against peace. Examples of war crimes were the order to kill commandos to the last man even if they surrendered, the use of prisoners for medical experiments and labour, the extermination of certain groups by organised mass murder, large scale deportation, the taking and shooting of hostages, the economic exploitation of occupied territories over and above the needs of the occupying troops, the devastation of towns and villages, the plunder of works of art. Examples of crimes against humanity were murder, extermination, enslavement, deportation, persecution and other inhumane acts committed against civilians. Examples of crimes against peace were planning, preparing, starting, or waging a war of aggression, or a war in violation of international treaties or agreements. As a result of the first trial, 12 Nazis were sentenced to death, seven got prison sentences, and three were acquitted. Since Nuremberg, Germany has strongly supported human rights. Nuremberg set up Germany's first Human Rights Office, and every two years presents the Nuremberg International Human Rights Award.

My opinion:

ISBN: 978-017023-077-3

Where terrorism fits with human rights

Think about identity, culture and organisation, and about continuity and change: how people define and seek human rights, and how the ideas and actions of people in the past have impacted on lives.

There is no legally binding or internationally accepted definition of **terrorism** although the United Nations defines it as 'any act intended to cause death or serious bodily harm to civilians or non-combatants with the purpose of intimidating a population or compelling a government or an international organisation to do or abstain from doing any act'. By acts such as assassination, bombing (car, bicycle, letter, parcel, petrol, pipe, sticky, suicide), arson, ambush, hijacking, cyber-terrorism and eco-terrorism, terrorists aim to cause terror among people and make them aware of terrorist individuals, groups and causes.

Practice 1

Choose words from the orange box to fill in the blanks in the following about what many experts say was the worst terrorist attack ever.

Skill: Identifying relationship
- Work out how objects, ideas, countries and people are connected; for example, what is the difference between Islam and Muslims?
- Use a pencil to fill in blanks until you are sure you are right. Cross off each word that you use from the box.

On September 11, 2001, which is now sometimes referred to as _____, 19 terrorists from the _____ group al-Qaeda hijacked four passenger jets after takeoffs from US airports. The hijackers flew two of the planes into the _____ of the World Trade Centre complex in _____ city and one plane into the _____ in Virginia. The fourth plane was supposed to hit another target but its passengers tried to take control of it and it crashed into a field in _____ Al-Qaeda said _____ support of _____, US troops in Saudi Arabia and _____ against _____ were causes of the attacks. Nearly 3,000 people died in the attacks; others were injured and exposed to _____ from collapsed buildings. Global stock markets and _____ dropped. Millions of people suffered symptoms of terror –_____ attacks, distress and dread. Leaders in most Middle Eastern countries and Afganistan _____ the attacks; Iraq said the US was reaping the fruits of its _____ against humanity. The US launched a _____ and invaded _____ to get rid of the Taliban which had harboured al-Qaeda members. Many countries strengthened anti-terrorist laws and airport _____. In some countries, especially the US, some _____ and South Asians became victims of _____ and harassment. People also targeted Sikhs because they associated Sikh _____ with Muslims. Muslim groups in the US condemned the attacks and asked Muslims to give skills and resources to help victims. Kiwi rock band _____ changed its name because Shihad was similar to the Arabic _____ which is sometimes used in reference to _____ war.

Afghanistan / anxiety / condemned / crimes / hate crimes / holy / Iraq / Islamic / Israel / jihad / Muslims / New York / 9/11 / Pentagon / Pennsylvania / sanctions / security / Shihad / tourism / toxins / turbans / Twin Towers / US / War on Terror

ISBN: 978-017023-077-3

Practice 2

Study the graph and make a list of your observations.

Skill: Activating prior knowledge
- Your observations should include everything from the obvious, such as the title, to the not-so-obvious such as the exact meaning of the title.
- Use the opportunity to show your skill with graph interpretation; for example, use terms such as x axis and y axis.

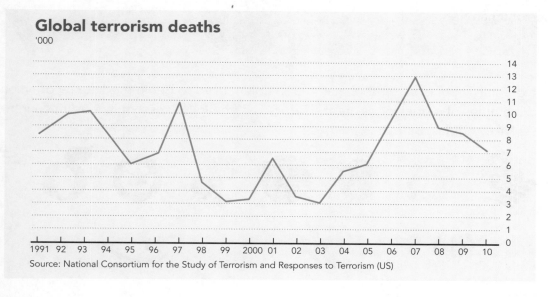

Global terrorism deaths
'000

Source: National Consortium for the Study of Terrorism and Responses to Terrorism (US)

ISBN: 978-0170-23-077-3

Interpreting logos

Think about identity, culture and organisation: how people seek human rights.

A **logo** is a graphic, sign, icon, symbol, name or emblem used to get immediate recognition from the public. Examples of global logos are the Red Cross (the Red Crescent in Muslim countries), McDonald's, Nike, Adidas, Batman.

Practice 1

Study the logo below and answer the questions about it.

Skill: Analysing
- Analysing is examining methodically and in detail. Here the task is easier because you have questions to guide you. If you put your answers together you would have an analysis.
- Always examine any extra information you are given. Here there is a caption which helps explain the logo's organisation.

*This is the logo of **Amnesty International**, the world's largest human rights organisation with thousands of supporters in New Zealand. The organisation began with an article about an appeal for amnesty - a pardon for real or perceived offences and especially political ones - for people who were imprisoned, tortured or awaiting execution because their opinions or religion were unacceptable to their governments; those governments were violating articles 18 and 19 of the Universal Declaration of Human Rights. Today its vision is a world where every person has all the rights in the Universal Declaration of Human Rights. It researches, documents and reports on human rights violations around the world and works to mobilise people to put pressure on governments and groups to stop the violations.*

1 Colours?_____

2 Ease of reproduction?_____

3 Impact?_____
_____

4 Proportions (size and shape)?_____
_____

5 Number of elements used?_____

ISBN: 978-017023-077-3

6 One image (element) used?_____

7 Second image used?_____

8 Which image communicates oppression? _____

9 How does it do that?_____
_____

10 Which image communicates hope?_____

11 How does it do that?_____
_____

12 Link with proverb 'Better to light a candle than curse the darkness'?_____
_____

13 Advantage of logo over initials AI or Amnesty International?_____
_____

14 Suitability (appropriateness to organisation)?_____
_____
_____

15 Durability (ability to last)?_____
_____

Practice 2

Study the logo below. Work out six criteria you could use to evaluate the logo. Then use your answers to the criteria to give it a mark out of 12.

An international competition called 'Logo for Human Rights' in 2011 attracted designs from people in just about every country. After an international jury had chosen the best ten, everyone in the world could vote online to find a winner. The winner was a Serbian designer who created the 'free as a man' logo based on a human hand and a bird in flight.

1 _____

2 _____

3 _____

4 _____

5 _____

6 _____

_____/12

ISBN: 978-017023-077-3

9 Linking business and human rights

Think about the economic world: how people's management of resources impacts on social sustainability.

Practice 1

Read Resource 1 and then give meanings for the words listed under it.

Skill: Comprehension

- This tests if you have generated meaning from the resource. Words can have different shades of meaning according to their context so always view the word in its context.
- Find the word in the text and highlight it. Then re-read the sentence in which it appears.

Resource 1 In 2011 the United Nations Human Rights Council adopted the Guiding Principles on Business and Human Rights, designed to provide for the first time a global standard for preventing and addressing the risk of adverse impacts on human rights linked to business activity. The Principles establish an authoritative global standard on the respective roles of businesses and governments in helping ensure that companies respect human rights in their own operations and through their business relationships. They elaborate on the three pillars of the UN Framework of Protect, Respect and Remedy. The three pillars are the state duty to protect against human rights abuses by third parties, including business, through appropriate policies, regulation, and adjudication; the corporate responsibility to respect human rights, that is, to act with due diligence to avoid infringing on the rights of others and address adverse impacts with which they are involved; and the need for greater access by victims to effective remedy, both judicial and non-judicial. They spell out the implications of the three pillars for governments, businesses and other stakeholders. They are applicable to all governments and to all businesses in all situations.

1 adopted ______________________

2 adverse ______________________

3 authoritative ______________________

4 pillars ______________________

5 appropriate ______________________

6 regulation ______________________

7 adjudication ______________________

8 corporate ______________________

9 due diligence ______________________

10 infringing ______________________

11 judicial ______________________

12 stakeholders ______________________

ISBN: 978-017023-077-3

Practice 2

Study the following resource and then supply the words from it which best suit the meanings given underneath it.

Skill: Supplying specific words
- Supply, as a key economic word, means the total amount of a good or service available; here supplying means making the words available by writing them in the correct place.
- As you supply a word highlight it in the resource. This will alert you that the word has already been supplied.

Resource 1 Economies and human rights are often entwined. Here are examples of areas experts say businesses from developed countries, looking to operate in developing countries, should try to make better.

The global financial crisis means many casual and temporary workers cannot join trade unions, or get employment benefits and contracts.	Although some products now carry a label showing consumers they were made without child labour, there are still an estimated 250 million child workers.
To support dissidents, bloggers, and writers, some IT companies have created tools such as encrypted technologies to bypass restrictions. Others have provided governments with surveillance technology to track down dissidents.	In areas such as the Middle East, South Asia, and sub-Saharan Africa, females have fewer human rights than males, yet research shows when females are educated and earning, society and economy improve.
Not consulting with groups likely to be affected by business does not allow locals to voice fears of impacts and business to respond to those fears. Not having grievance mechanisms in place for locals to go increases public protests and conflict.	Land acquisition and use by business, especially in Sub-Saharan Africa, is increasing. Land-grabbing can harm locals through actions such as evictions and prevent them from benefitting economically and sustainably.
Corruption, such as contracts going to highest bidders, shoddy work that threatens the health and safety of workers, extortion of bribes, and lack of transparency leads to human rights abuses.	Some developing countries are emerging from conflict. In places like South Sudan, Libya and Myanmar, changing politics means scope for investments but also for new tensions.

1 people opposed to official policy _____ _____

2 forced out _____ _____

3 real or imagined wrong or complaint _____ _____

4 close observation _____ _____

5 dishonest conduct by those in power _____ _____

6 not regular _____ _____

7 obtaining through force or threats _____ _____

8 operating in open manner _____ _____

9 region south of Sahara Desert _____ _____

10 for future generations as well _____ _____

11 put into what offers potential rewards _____ _____

12 converted into cipher or code _____ _____

13 limitations and controls _____ _____

14 buyers and users _____ _____

15 systems and processes _____ _____

16 worldwide _____ _____

ISBN: 978-017023-077-3

Teamwork in action

Think about identity, culture, and organisation: how people seek human rights.

The freedom to work with others in a team is a basic human right and one that will become increasingly important in solving the problems of the future.

Practice 1

Highlight in one colour features from the following that belong to members of a team and highlight with another colour features that belong to members of a group who are not acting as a team.

Skill: Concept-formations
- This is organising information about an entity, and associating it with the label – here it is teamwork.
- Think of teamwork as combined action by a group of people where individuals recognise all individuals have importance and are willing to put the unity and success of the group ahead of their personal interests to work towards a common goal.

Listen to each other and feel comfortable expressing opinions.	Work independently.	Are hesitant to give opinions.
	Realise goals are met best by supporting each other.	
Encouraged to share skills and knowledge.	Trust the motives of others.	Work collaboratively.
Do not always support each other.	Are threatened by arguments and allow resentment to build up as problems are not solved.	
Are allocated tasks and duties by the leader who may not encourage suggestions.	Have not personally invested in the project as they have not been closely involved in planning.	
Take little or no part in decision-making and resent the leader's power.	Have a sense of ownership in the project as they have been involved in creating goals.	
Reluctant to contribute because they are unsure of their relationships with others.	Uncertain when targets are reached as goals are not concisely expressed.	
Are not always respectful.	Expected to conform.	Show respect for each other.
Do not always trust the motives of others.	Encouraged to think outside the square.	Don't always work towards the same goal.
Take part in decision-making while recognising the leader may need to have the casting vote.	Are confident in the knowledge that the leader welcomes suggestions to best use skills and experience of members.	
Know when the goal is reached as it was expressed clearly from the outset.	Work towards a common goal.	Enjoy working with others and up for any challenge.
Resolve conflict by positive problem-solving.	Unwilling to share information.	

ISBN: 978-017023-077-3

Practice 2

Skill: Setting goals
- This asks you to consider goals set by others and by yourself.
- Goal-setting is to do with the future and provides vision and motivation.
- Refer back to Practice 1 to refresh your thinking.

Read the following and answer the questions about it.

People charged with investigating reports of human rights violations have to act as a team to achieve the goal which is to make sure they have done everything possible to prove or disprove the allegations. They will search for physical evidence provided by articles involved in the event, such as electrical cables used for whipping, bullets recovered from the site of a massacre, a blouse covered in blood worn by a victim. They will look for demonstrative evidence which are articles that demonstrate, such as a sketch of the pattern on an arm that cigarette burns made, or a map of the route taken by a bus to get to a village to be raided drawn by a child who was used as a human shield by being placed at the bus window among rebels to discourage defenders from shooting at the bus. They will also hunt out any documentary evidence, which are original documents like emails, letters, hospital charts and medical records, diaries, photographs and videos, which might show a person being tortured during detention, or soldiers shooting civilians. They will also search for testimonial evidence which consists of a person's own words told orally, in writing, or by video such as in taped audio interviews, video interviews, and written accounts.

1   Name the four categories of evidence a team will search for and give an example of each.

_____

_____

_____

_____

_____

_____

2   Explain the message of the images.

_____

_____

_____

3   You are to lead a team of six people visiting a country to investigate recent allegations of stonings. State six things you will concentrate on to ensure the team is a well-oiled machine.

   a _____

   b _____

   c _____

   d _____

   e _____

   f _____

ISBN: 978-0170-23-077-3

11 How public opinion polls work

Think about identity, culture and organisation: how people define and seek human rights.

One way people check on human rights issues that affect society is to carry out **public opinion polls**.

Skill: Identifying errors
- Activity 1 does not tell if there are errors or not; consider the statement and then find something in the text that either proves or disproves it.
- Activity 2 tells you there are errors; use what you know about the correct way to present graphs to help identify the errors.

Practice 1

Read the following and do the activities under it.

A public opinion poll, usually called a poll and sometimes a survey or questionnaire, is an inquiry into public opinion conducted by interviewing a random sample of people usually either in person or by phone. A straw poll is an unofficial one. Gallup Polls (the name comes from its American founder George Gallup) are carried out regularly in over 140 countries around the world, including New Zealand, representing 95 percent of the world's adult population. The media often quotes them because experts consider them reliable and objective. Gallup publishes results, analyses and videos daily on the web and conducts polls on nearly every political, social and economic issue of the day including controversial subjects. Probability sampling, such as simple random sampling, is the basis for poll research. The idea is that all individuals in a population have an equal chance of being selected and that a small percent of a population can represent the attitudes, opinions, or projected behaviour of all people. For example, in 2010 Gallup's global snapshot of wellbeing used data collected in 155 countries or areas since 2005. Using the Cantril Self-Anchoring Striving Scale and asking respondents to rate their current and future lives from 0 being the worst possible to 10 being the best possible, the poll classified respondents as thriving, struggling or suffering. The poll showed a vast division in economic development around the world. The percentage who were thriving ranged from 82 in Denmark to 1 in Togo. New Zealand and Australia were ranked in Asia; New Zealand was the top thriver at 63 percent and Australia tied for second with Israel at 62 percent; Cambodia was bottom with 3 percent. The Median Percentage Thriving by Region was Americas 42, Europe 29, Asia 17, Africa 8.

ISBN: 978-017023-077-3

1 Highlight **T** (for True) or **F** (for False) for each of the following statements.

   T   **F**   Gallup Polls take place in New Zealand.

   T   **F**   Experts consider Gallup Polls to be biased.

   T   **F**   Polls are not used to guage how people might act in the future.

   T   **F**   Random sampling aims to come up with the same results that would have been obtained had every single member of a population been interviewed.

   T   **F**   Respondent is another term for 'global'.

   T   **F**   One word to describe the Cantril Self-Anchoring Striving Scale could be ladder.

   T   **F**   A table to show the Median Percentage Thriving by Region of the 2010 Gallup Poll would name five regions.

2 The person who created this fictitious poll result to use as an example made at least five errors. Show these by writing on the graph.

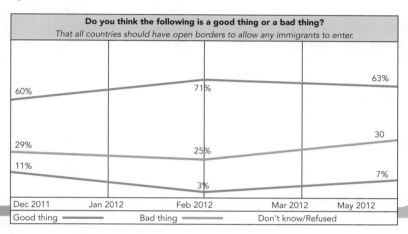

Do you think the following is a good thing or a bad thing?
That all countries should have open borders to allow any immigrants to enter.

60% — 71% — 63%

29% — 25% — 30

11% — 3% — 7%

Dec 2011   Jan 2012   Feb 2012   Mar 2012   May 2012

Good thing ━━━━   Bad thing ━ ━ ━   Don't know/Refused

Practice 2

Carry out your own poll of five to ten people.

Skill: Oral discourse
- Make a list of respondents and decide how you will carry out the poll.
- Explain to people the reason for the poll and ask if they would be willing to take part.
- Speak clearly and give people time to think of their responses.

Do you think the following is a good thing or a bad thing for the country?

That the drinking age be raised to 21.

	Yes	No	Don't know/Refused
Name _____	☐ Yes	☐ No	☐ Don't know/Refused
Name _____	☐ Yes	☐ No	☐ Don't know/Refused
Name _____	☐ Yes	☐ No	☐ Don't know/Refused
Name _____	☐ Yes	☐ No	☐ Don't know/Refused
Name _____	☐ Yes	☐ No	☐ Don't know/Refused
Name _____	☐ Yes	☐ No	☐ Don't know/Refused
Name _____	☐ Yes	☐ No	☐ Don't know/Refused
Name _____	☐ Yes	☐ No	☐ Don't know/Refused
Name _____	☐ Yes	☐ No	☐ Don't know/Refused
Name _____	☐ Yes	☐ No	☐ Don't know/Refused

ISBN: 978-017023-077-3

12 Awareness of entrepreneurship and enterprise

Think about the economic world: how people seek economic growth through business, enterprise and innovation.

Practice 1

Study Resources 1 and 2 and do the following.

1 Highlight qualities you have that would help you become an entrepreneur.
2 Tick the examples you have heard of and double tick three you would choose to research for a project.

Skill: Self-knowledge and self-control

- This is about being aware of and analysing your own thinking processes and learning.
- To practise and learn this skill you have to be honest with yourself.
- There are no 'right' or 'wrong' answers here.

Resource 1: People with entrepreneurship and enterprise have many of the following qualities which help them succeed in business.

initiative (act and take charge before others do)		ambition	boldness	risk-taking
accepting responsibility for actions	wish to be self-employed		ability to diversify	
resourcefulness (ability to cope with difficult situations)			desire to improve conditions	
desire to address some global social and economic conditions such as poverty				
wish to get a balance between work and leisure		desire for economic change		
innovation (introducing new technologies)		imagination	visualisation	
desire to earn a living doing something they love		recognition of opportunities		
divergent thinking (having new and complex ideas)			courage	creativity
convergent thinking (evaluating, analysing, choosing the best idea)				productivity
interest in new solutions	problem-solving	determination	efficiency	patience

Resource 2: Examples of people with enterprise and entrepreneurship

Bruce Plested, NZ, Mainfreight	Richard Branson, UK, Virgin	Henry Ford, US, cars
Carmel Fisher, NZ, Fund manager	Victoria Ransom, NZ, Wildfire	Walt Disney, US, movies
Wendy Pye, NZ, publisher	Estee Lauder, US, cosmetics	Trelise Cooper, NZ, fashion
Michael Hill, NZ, jewellery	Rovio Mobile, Finland, Angry Birds	Peter Jackson, NZ, film production
Stephen Tindall , NZ, Warehouse	Anita Roddick, UK, Body Shop	Simon Cowel, UK, promoter
Lee Mathias, NZ, Birthcare	Sharon Hunter, NZ, PC Direct	Peter Maire, NZ, Navman
Sam Morgan, NZ, Trade Me	Bill Buckley, NZ, silicon chips	Karen Walker, NZ, fashion
Oprah Winfrey, US, entertainment	Bill Gates, US, Microsoft	P. T. Barnum, US, circus

Practice 2

Study Resource 3 and highlight advice you would find easy and worthwhile to follow.

Skill: Self-knowledge and self-control
- Read closely; for example, you may have good ideas but do you think you would be passionate about them?
- As you read the advice, consider how it might help you in life even if you were not interested in becoming an entrepreneur.

Resource 3: Advice from successful entrepreneurs		
Keep a journal about ideas, problems, thoughts, observations.		Learn how to listen.
Join online entrepreneur forums and discussion groups.		Learn how to work in a team.
Research techniques such as concept-mapping.		Be open to ideas from other people.
Talk to people who have started their own businesses.		Start your own business.
Don't be afraid to dream.	Be enthusiastic.	Be passionate about your ideas.
Realise you need to keep trying after you fail.		Keep senses open to new experiences.
Practise being creative in response to changes and challenges.		Be energetic.
Find something you love to do and make it a business.		Make a solid business plan.
Have good relationships with people.		Treat others as you want to be treated.
Research techniques such as relaxation and meditation.		Keep up with technology.
Do market research to see if your dream could work.		Learn to communicate clearly.
Try to be positive rather than negative; see the cup as half-full rather than half-empty.		
Read newspapers.		Keep up with current affairs..

Appreciating Kiwi ingenuity

Think about the economic world: how people seek economic growth through business, innovation and enterprise.

Before instant communication and fast travel, New Zealand was distant from the rest of the world. This helped start the tradition of Kiwi ingenuity where people used creativity, originality and innovation to solve problems and meet challenges. In 1900 New Zealand had the highest number of patent applications per capita in the world. Number 8 wire, a guage of fencing wire, became a symbol for Kiwi ingenuity because Kiwis adapted it for so many other uses.

Practice 1

Choose your own system to show the match between the description of the innovation in column 2 of the chart with the Kiwi innovator and name of the innovation in column 1.

Skill: Matching
- This means finding how two things correspond in some essential way.
- Use your Kiwi ingenuity; for example 'Aquada' contains 'aqua' which shows you need to find something do to with water.
- Always do the familiar first.
- Consider systems you could use (colours? arrows? numbers?) and decide which one would work best for you to show your matching.

Glenn Martin: jet pack	produces sawn timber in one operation
Colin Murdoch: disposable syringe	discovery of nuclear fission
Colin Murdoch: tranquiliser dart gun	revolutionised wool industry
Alan Gibbs: Aquada	jumping while connected to structure by cord
Ernest Rutherford: atom-splitting	fast securing and releasing of ships
Harry Wigley: retractable plane skis	mini-farthing folding electric motorcycle
Paul Beckett: blokart	world-record-setting machine
A.J.Hackett: modern bungy	giant ball that spins down hills
Ernest Godward: economiser	protective plastic strip for car rims
Arthur Lydiard: jogging	revolutionised beer brewing
Keith Alexander: spring-free trampoline	controls animal movement
William Atack: referee's whistle	throwaway that prevents contamination
Akers brothers: Zorb	deodorised cream in butter
Warren Tatham: Sushezi	extracts air from freezer bags
Deborah & Chris Chester: RimPro-Tec	boils water outdoors on open fire
Joy Allock: Word Detective game	fertilised paddocks
Grant Ryan: YikeBike	low-geared to climb hills
Bill & Henry Gallagher: electric fence	to catch, examine and release animals
Norma McCulloch: hand pump	enables fliers to stay aloft for half an hour
John Hart: thermette	kite-powered snow travel
Leon Styles: paintball operation systems	glacier and snow landings
Peter Montgomery: vacuum mooring	building up physical fitness
Alan Pritchard: aerial topdressing	keeps children safe during exercise
Johnny Callender: farm bike	helps English literacy

ISBN: 978-0-170230773-3

Godfrey Bowen: better shearing technique	early car carburettor
John Britten: Britten motorcyle	refined marine jet propulsion
Bill Hamilton: modern jetboat	keeping children safe during games
Lamont Murray & Frank Board: Vacreator	transforms car to boat at touch of a button
Peter Lynn: tipping blade portable sawmill	home-made sushi
Peter Lynn: KiteSled	tagging as an extreme sport
Morton Coutts: continuous fermentation	three-wheeled land yacht

Practice 2

Skill: Decision-making
- This asks you to use self-knowledge to help you make a decision.
- Use the resources to ask yourself key questions such as, Might I have the desire and ability to break away from the mob?

Use the resources to help you decide if you might have Kiwi ingenuity, now or in the future. Write a few sentences explaining your decision.

Resource 1

Discovery Alteration
Inspiration Creativity
Technology Idea Experiment
Change
Innovation
Research Improvement
Development Analysis
Concept Invention
Decision Prototype Science

Resource 3

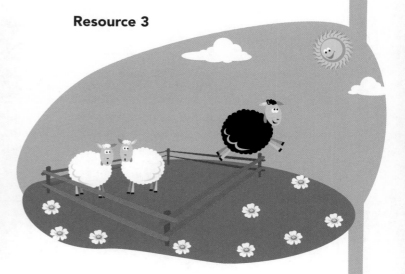

Resource 2 Sir Ray Avery is a Kiwi self-made millionaire. His inventions help millions of people throughout the developing world. He says his motivation to help others stems from his abusive childhood, and his Kiwi can-do attitude. He and his team visit hospitals in developing countries. They work out what the hospitals need, such as an incubator to save babies or an intra-ocular lens to restore sight, and invent something to do the job cheaply and efficiently. In New Zealand they find people who can help create the invention. For example, someone might mention that someone else has something in his garage that might help. Ray Avery and his team don't get paid.

_____

_____

_____

_____

_____

_____

ISBN: 978-0-17023-077-3

14 Looking at the future

Think about the economic world: how people seek economic growth through business, enterprise, and innovation.

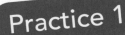

Practice 1

Study the chart below and fill in the missing data to show how work is changing.

> **Skill: Assessing past, present and future**
> - This asks you to evaluate and estimate by considering data that has been supplied (alongside the missing data).
> - Assess in terms of what you have observed in your society such as thinking how older generations in your family regarded work before the days of instant communication. For example, instead of working across time and space, people regarded work as being a physical place to go to for the day, such as a factory or office.

past work	(present work)	future work
People leave home in the morning to go to their places of work for the day and return home after work.	People work across time and space in virtual teams. Team members can be anywhere in the world.	
Slow communication eg. landline phones, snail mail.		
Call centres are huge offices in rural areas or developing countries like India.		
	Job-sharing allows leisure time.	
One manager makes decisions.		
People in a company have all met each other.		
	People are from different backgrounds so team leaders have to be culturally aware.	
	Female management essential and different to male eg. focus more on long term, more concerned with fosterng good working relationships among team members, motivational.	
Jobs available for most who want them.		
No business consideration for environment and factors such as climate change.		
	Consideration of sustainability creates jobs in industries that sustain Earth.	
Long or life-time work at one company.		
	Feelings of success from you getting what matters to you eg. seeing the colleague you mentor win a prize, or taking summers off for surfing.	

ISBN: 978-017023-077-3

Companies expect employees to work set hours on set days.	
Corner-cutting scandals eg. lead-paint-contaminated children's toys and melamine-laced milk in China.	
	Robots and androids do manual tasks.
Workers do not expect much change in technology.	
	People do not gain identity through their work; they consider other things important.

Practice 2

Choose one of the following images and explain how it relates to the future of work.

Skill: Selecting
- This asks you to determine which is the best or most suitable to kick-start your ideas.
- Think about which one you most identify with or with which you have the most immediate connection.
- Look again at the chart in Practice 1 to help you explain the image.

Digital identity.

Female android.

Internet business.

Futuristic greenhouse.

Phone social network.

_____

_____

_____

_____

_____

_____

ISBN: 978-0170-23-077-3

Think about place and environment: how people move between places.

Practice 1

ISBN: 978-017023-077-3

Skill: Critical thinking
- This means analysing material carefully and reaching sound conclusions. For example, is Resource 1 most closely linked to a social reason, a politcal reason or an economic reason?
- Consider how each could contribute information; for example, the headline in Resource 4 is a clever play on words; maybe you could use it in your introduction as an example of media attention.

Study the resources below about New Zealanders moving to Australia. In the blank boxes under each make notes on how you could use each resource for a research project on the topic.

Resource 1

1860s: many Australians come to new goldfields in New Zealand

1880s: many Kiwis move to Australia to get away from New Zealand economic depression

Late 1960s: more prevalent and cheaper air travel draws Kiwis to Australia

1976 – 1982: 103,000 Kiwis move to Australia to escape economic recession

1987: Kiwi movement to Australia increases because of sharemarket crash

1998: Kiwis leave for Australia because of Asian financial crisis and New Zealand drought

2000s: 1 in 9 Kiwis live in Australia; 2001: 96,000 draw Australian welfare

2006 – 9: Kiwi movement to Australia increases because of Australian economic boom

2008: Kiwi movement to Australia increases because of global financial crisis

Year to April 2012: 53,237: Kiwis move to Australia

Resource 2: In the 1990s many non-New Zealand-born living in New Zealand saw New Zealand as 'a back door' into Australia. The number of them moving to Australia grew from 960 a year to nearly 10,000.

Resource 3: A famous quote, attributed to a New Zealand Prime Minister, is that New Zealanders who go to Australia raise the IQ of both countries.

Resource 4: Newspaper headline: **KIWIS DITCHING NEW ZEALAND FOR AUSTRALIA**

Resource 5: Over 600,000 Kiwis live in Australia. About 65,000 Australians live in New Zealand.

Resource 6: Number out of each 1000 who moved to Australia June 2011-June 2012

Auckland	10.00	Christchurch	11.50	Gisborne	13.73
Kaikoura	14.00	Opotiki	13.40	Porirua	13.24
Rotorua	13.59	South Waikato	13.62	Tauranga	13.75
Wairoa	13.41	Whakatane	13.50	Whangarei	13.51

Resource 7: Kiwis moving to Australia (March years)

Cities	2009/10	2011/12	Cities	2009/10	2011/12
Auckland	9486	15005	Nelson	222	402
Christchurch	1892	4320	Palmerston North	387	712
Dunedin	532	894	Rotorua	515	937
Gisborne	318	640	Tauranga	822	1593
Hamilton	987	1565	Wellington	2519	4453
Hastings	465	773	Whangarei	537	1088

Resource 8: Pull factors of Australia - warmer climate, larger cities for more night-life, similar culture, better lifestyle, more jobs, better working conditions, bigger salaries, friends and family already there, lack of earthquakes, promises of cash bonuses, more sport opportunities.

Practice 2

Now study the resources again and highlight 10 things you could research further to add depth to your research project.

Skill: Assessing current knowledge
- This asks you to look at resources and evaluate what you do or do not know or understand. For example, which sectors in Australia have been promising cash bonuses as a lure to Kiwis?
- Consider what might be helpful to find out. For example, might it be helpful to find out which goldfields drew the Australian miners and if they stayed after the rushes had ended?

ISBN: 978-0170-23-077-3

Examining statistical data

Think about place and environment: that people move between places.

Practice 1

Study the two graphs below and list 10 similarities.

Skill: Interpreting graphic data
- The data here has been arranged graphically to make it easier and quicker to understand it.
- Note that countries collect statistics on and count numbers of immigrants in varying ways and it is difficult to harmonise them across countries.
- Remember that a migrant moves from one place to another, which can include one country to another, and an immigrant moves from one country to another.

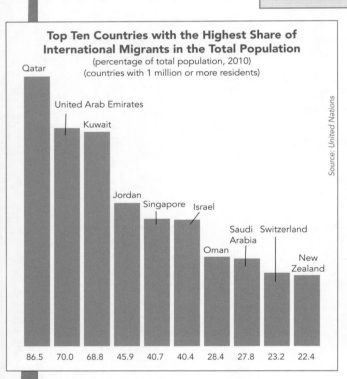

Top Ten Countries with the Highest Share of International Migrants in the Total Population
(percentage of total population, 2010)
(countries with 1 million or more residents)

Qatar — 86.5
United Arab Emirates — 70.0
Kuwait — 68.8
Jordan — 45.9
Singapore — 40.7
Israel — 40.4
Oman — 28.4
Saudi Arabia — 27.8
Switzerland — 23.2
New Zealand — 22.4

Source: United Nations

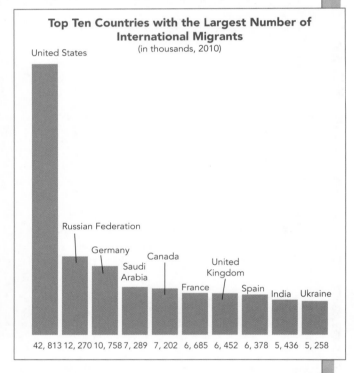

Top Ten Countries with the Largest Number of International Migrants
(in thousands, 2010)

United States — 42, 813
Russian Federation — 12, 270
Germany — 10, 758
Saudi Arabia — 7, 289
Canada — 7, 202
France — 6, 685
United Kingdom — 6, 452
Spain — 6, 378
India — 5, 436
Ukraine — 5, 258

1 _____
2 _____
3 _____
4 _____
5 _____
6 _____
7 _____
8 _____
9 _____
10 _____

ISBN: 978-0170230-077-3

Practice 2

Study the tables and answer the questions that follow. You may need to refer back to the Practice 1 graphs.

Resource 1: Most Populous Countries 2010

Rank	Country	Population (000)
1	China	1,347,380
2	India	1,184,130
3	US	310,207
4	Indonesia	243,001
5	Brazil	201,122
6	Pakistan	179,674
7	Bangladesh	158,067
8	Nigeria	152,198
9	Russia	139,387
10	Japan	126,835
	Global migrants	215,764

Resource 2: New Zealand's Migrants 2010

Stock of immigrants: 962.1 thousand
Stock of immigrants as % of population: 22.4%
Females as % of immigrants: 52.4%
Refugees as % of immigrants: 0.4%
Top source countries: UK, China, Australia, Samoa, India, South Africa, Fiji, Republic of Korea, Netherlands, Tonga

Resource 3: Survey of Immigrants to New Zealand 2010

75.7 % were employed.
69.8 % of employed worked in a skilled job.
84.9 % of employed were either satisfied or very satisfied with their main job.
70.6 % had enough or more than enough money to meet their everyday needs.
51.9 % owned or partly owned their dwelling.
49.3 % lived in the Auckland region.
31.5 % lived in the rest of the North Island.
More than 9 out of 10 were either satisfied or very satisfied with life in NZ.
76.0 % felt either safe or very safe in NZ.
78.4 % had gained or intended to apply for NZ citizenship.

1 If 'global migrants' was a country, what number would it be ranked in Resource 1? _____

2 Of the most populous countries how many are in the top 10 for having the largest number of international migrants? Name them.
_____

3 What percentage of New Zealand immigrants are males?_____

4 Are the top source countries for New Zealand's immigrants likely or not likely to produce refugees? Give a reason for your answer. _____
_____

5 Which country is most likely to be the one that experts say may soon become the most populous? Give a reason for your answer. _____
_____

6 Of New Zealand's top source countries, how many are the most populous? Name them.
_____

7 Which table or graph best shows that New Zealand has a high intake of immigrants? Explain your answer. _____
_____

8 What does populous mean?_____
_____

9 Of New Zealand's top source countries, how many are Asian? Name them. _____
_____

10 How many are in Oceania? Name them._____
_____

11 Suggest a reason that up-to-date statistics for migrants are rarely available. _____
_____

12 What percentage of immigrants lived in the South Island? _____

13 Generally, are immigrants pleased or displeased with their move to New Zealand?_____

14 What percentage of employed immigrants were in unskilled work?_____

15 How many topics are addressed in the survey results?_____

ISBN: 978-0170-230773-3

17 How to create captions

Think about place and environment: that people move between places.

A caption is text that appears with an image in places like a web-page or newspaper. It can be a few words or several sentences although must always be clear and informative. As it is one of the most commonly-read pieces in an article, it needs to draw you in and encourage you to read the article.

Practice 1

Explain whether the caption is appropriate for the image below.

Skill: Critical thinking
- This asks you to focus on deciding about suitability.
- The caption is taken from a poem engraved inside the pedestal of the Statue of Liberty, and its definition of immigrants is often quoted. Does it add interest to and curiosity about the image? Does it explain sufficiently what the image is about?
- Use the skill tips in Practice 2 to help.

'Give me your tired, your poor, Your huddled masses yearning to breathe free, The wretched refuse of your teeming shore. Send these, the homeless, tempest-tost to me...'.

_____
_____
_____
_____
_____
_____
_____
_____
_____
_____
_____
_____
_____

ISBN 978-0170230773

Practice 2

Use the key words in brackets under the images to help you write captions to go with the images.

(Boat people immigrants)

_____

_____

_____

(Migration to the Wild West)

_____

_____

_____

(19th century immigrants)

_____

_____

_____

(Refugees)

_____

_____

_____

(Illegal immigration)

_____

_____

_____

_____

ISBN: 978-017-023-077-3

Honing graph skills

Think about place and environment: that people move between places.

Practice 1

Study Resources 1 and 2 and complete the activities that accompany them.

Make four comments about what this graph shows.

Skill: Analysing graphs
- This asks you to clarify the graphs by examining their parts and their relationships.
- Concentrate on what data the graphs show; don't talk about construction, such as what type of graphs they are.
- The title of a graph is a good place to start.

Resource 1

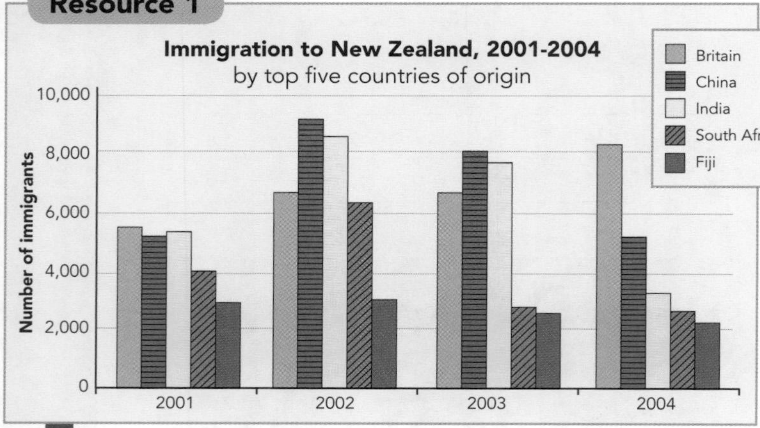

Immigration to New Zealand, 2001-2004
by top five countries of origin

Legend: Britain, China, India, South Africa, Fiji

Y-axis: Number of immigrants (0 to 10,000)
X-axis: 2001, 2002, 2003, 2004

_____
_____
_____
_____
_____
_____
_____
_____
_____

Make four comments about what this graph shows.

Resource 2

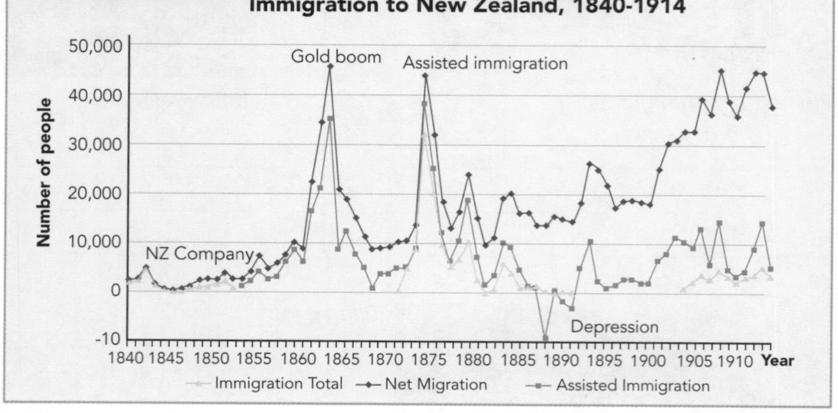

Immigration to New Zealand, 1840-1914

Y-axis: Number of people (-10 to 50,000)
X-axis: Year 1840 1845 1850 1855 1860 1865 1870 1875 1880 1885 1890 1895 1900 1905 1910

Labels: NZ Company, Gold boom, Assisted immigration, Depression

Legend: Immigration Total, Net Migration, Assisted Immigration

_____
_____
_____
_____

ISBN: 978-0170-23-077-3

Practice 2

Study Resources 3 and 4 and complete the activities that accompany them.

Make four comments about what this graph shows.

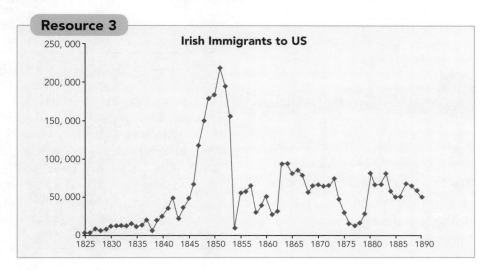

Resource 3

Irish Immigrants to US

_____

_____

_____

_____

Make four comments about what this graph shows.

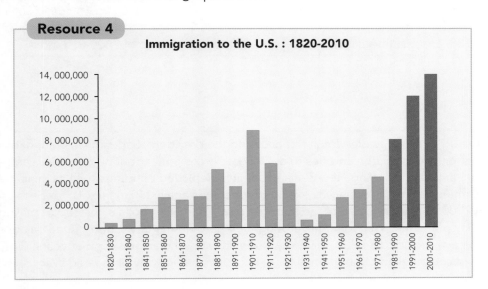

Resource 4

Immigration to the U.S. : 1820-2010

_____

_____

_____

_____

ISBN: 978-017023-077-3

Revising tables and visuals

Think about place and environment and the economic world: that people move between places and how economic decisions impact on people, communities and nations.

Practice 1

Highlight information that should appear in a table about the number of Mozzies in Australian states and in a table about one day's spending on the war of Iraq. In the space under the text describe what the finished tables would look like.

Skill: Visualising
- This asks you to see the finished product in your mind, rather than actually construct it.
- A table contains data only; ignore any commentary on the data such as how accurate it is or background information.
- Picture the table by working out how many columns it has, what the headings of the columns are and in what order they are arranged.

Maori in Australia (Mozzies) are the new migration. Australian census figures put the country's 2011 population at 21.5 million. 128,418 were Maori, a 38 percent increase on 2006. Some experts say the figure could be 150,000 Mozzies as Maori are likely to be under-counted because of the way the census is structured. Australian Capital Territory has the lowest numbers – 711 in 2006 and 916 in 2011, making a 28.8 percent growth. Tasmania had 877 in 2006 and 1074 in 2011 with a 22.5 percent growth. Queensland claims the most Maori with 48,282, a 55.4 percent increase on the 31,077 in 2006. Western Australia saw the greatest leap in Mozzies with 23,062 in 2011 up by 83.7 percent from 12,557. New South Wales had the lowest percent growth with 8.0, going from 29,816 in 2006 to 32,192 in 2011. Victoria's figures of 14,265 in 2006 and 18,366 in 2011 gave it a 28.7 percent growth, similar to Northern Territory's 28.2 percent that came from an increase of 1005 to 1288, and South Australia's 24.3 percent from an increase of 2606 to 3238.

In 2003 the US and UK invaded Iraq after accusing the president, Saddam Hussein, of having weapons of mass destruction and ties to al-Qaeda. Forces from about 30 countries came in to help the US and UK, including New Zealand soldiers deployed on duties such as mine-clearing. Conflict continued after Hussein was executed for crimes against humanity. US experts estimated that from 2003 to 2011 one day of the Iraq War cost 720 million dollars. Instead of paying for a war, one day of the Iraq War could have bought 84 new elementary schools. One day of the Iraq War could have provided 34,904 university students with scholarships for four years. One day of the Iraq War could have bought homes for 6,482 families. One day of the Iraq War could have provided renewable energy for 1,274,336 homes.

ISBN: 978-017023-077-3

Examine the two visuals, which show the same information – top 10 share of world military spending (2010) – and write a few sentences about which visual you think does the best job and why.

Top 10 Share of World Military Spending 2010

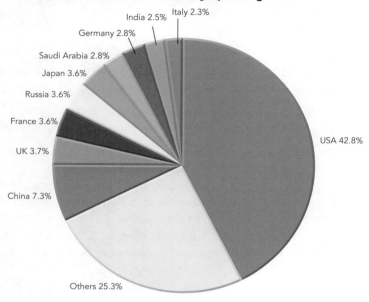

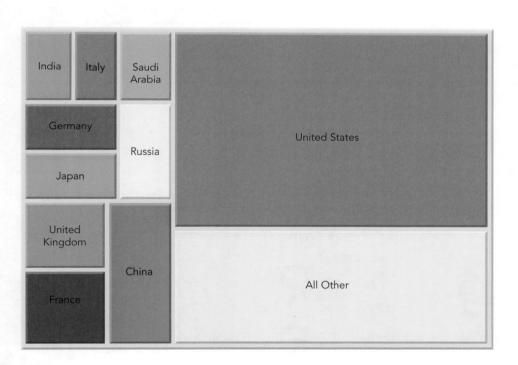

_____

_____

_____

_____

_____

ISBN: 978-0170-23-077-3

20 Understanding future problem-solving

Think about place and environment: how people move between places and how this has effects on people and places.

Future Problem Solving (FPS) was founded by American creativity pioneer Dr Torrance and involves thousands of students annually from many countries including New Zealand. Set topics often involve people's relationships with the environment such as Coral Reefs, Green Living, Water Quality, Environmental Law, and Climate Change, all of which can be causes of people moving between places.

Practice 1

Study the FPS process and images, and decide which image best illustrates FPS. Circle the image and explain why you chose it.

Skill: Decision-making and explaining
- Make sure you understand the FPS process first. To reinforce your understanding you could underline key words, such as **find**, **judge**.
- Then work out what the images are saying. There is no right or wrong answer here and one image might suddenly shine brightly for you.
- In your explanation show how you link the image to the process, such as 'Future problem-solving is about unravelling problems that create knots in the world ...'

The six steps of the FPS process
1 Find possible challenges and problems.
2 Decide what is the most important or underlying problem.
3 Think of solutions to solve the problem.
4 Decide on criteria by which to judge the solutions.
5 Judge solutions, and determine which is the best overall.
6 Elaborate on this solution to make a plan to put it into action.

ISBN: 978-0-17023-077-3

Practice 2

Your FPS team has the following resources. Make notes under them that you could contribute to team discussions.

Number of people in Kiribati: 113,000
Islands of Kiribati: 32 atolls and 1 raised coral island
Height of atolls: none is over 3m above sea level
Size of Kiribati: 3,500,000 sq km
Location: only country in the world in all 4 hemispheres
Name of people from Kiribati: i-Kiribati

Global warming has caused rising sea levels. Some atolls have begun to disappear. Some villagers have had to leave homes. Salt water has ruined some freshwater supplies and crops. Storms cause shoreline erosion. Experts say Kiribati could be the first country in the world which loses its country to rising sea levels, causing its people to become environmental refugees. If such refugees have skills to offer they become more attractive immigrants. Kiribati is a member of the Alliance of Small Island States, an organisation of low-lying coastal and small island countries vulnerable to rising sea levels. The Alliance aims to make sure such countries have a say on ways to address global warming.

Blast fishing with dynamite and grenades damages coral reefs. Replanting mangroves and strengthening laws could reduce coastal erosion. Water management around the capital Tarawa could be improved. One idea proposed has been to build man-made islands like oil-rigs for people to live on.

In 2008, Kiribati officials asked New Zealand and Australia to accept Kiribati citizens as permanent refugees and in 2012 were negotiating to buy land in Fiji to relocate people.

ISBN: 978-0170-23-077-3

Defining Pacific Rim and Pacific Basin

Think about place and environment: that people move between places which has results such as economic growth.

Pacific Rim = nations around the edges of the Pacific Ocean.

Pacific Basin = Pacific Rim nations and island nations in the Pacific Ocean.

The Pacific Ocean takes up about a third of Earth's surface and has been the scene of much human movement since prehistoric time such as Polynesians from the Asian Pacific Rim. In recent years, many countries and regions have modernised their economies such as the Four Asian Tigers (Hong Kong, South Korea, Singapore and Taiwan) and the Tiger Cubs (Indonesia, Malaysia, Philippines and Thailand). Tokyo, Los Angeles, and Hong Kong are world financial centres. Much of the world's shipping goes through this area, especially between China and the United States.

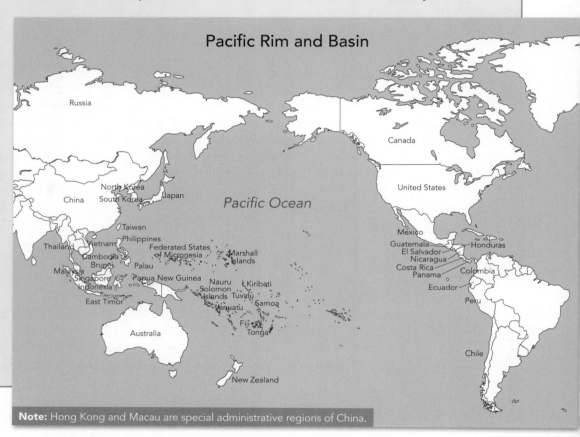

Pacific Rim and Basin

Note: Hong Kong and Macau are special administrative regions of China.

Practice 1

Use the map to help you do the following.

1 Colour nations in the Americas one colour. (13)

2 Colour nations in Oceania another colour. (14)

3 Colour nations in Asia another colour. (15)

4 How many nations are there in the Pacific Basin?_____

Skill: Identifying relationships

- This means recognising ways in which elements, in this case nations, are related.
- Think logically; for example Americas will mean North America, Central America and South America.

ISBN: 978-017023-077-3

5 Write a definition of the Pacific Basin for a web dictionary. _____

_____

6 Explain why Hong Kong and Hawaii are not named on the map. _____

_____

7 Give a reason this area is important to New Zealand. _____

_____

8 Give a reason the area is concerned with climate change. _____

_____

9 Name two ways goods and people move around the area. _____

_____

10 Of the islands in the Pacific which one do you think was most likely to be the last to be peopled?
Give a reason for your answer. _____

_____

Practice 2

Learn the names and locations of the nations in the Pacific Rim and Basin. When you are confident, cover up the map in Practice 1 and put the names on to the blank map.

Skill: Remembering

- This involves a conscious effort to store and retrieve information, a useful skill even though you live in a digital age. If you were reading an article or story set in the Pacific Basin, or were present at a high-powered meeting about Pacific economies, being able to visualise where all the places were would save you having to constantly check on your iPad or iPhone for the locations.
- Concentration is a key factor here. Start with New Zealand.
- Playing interactive net games such as Sporcle will quickly help you store in your head the locations of places.

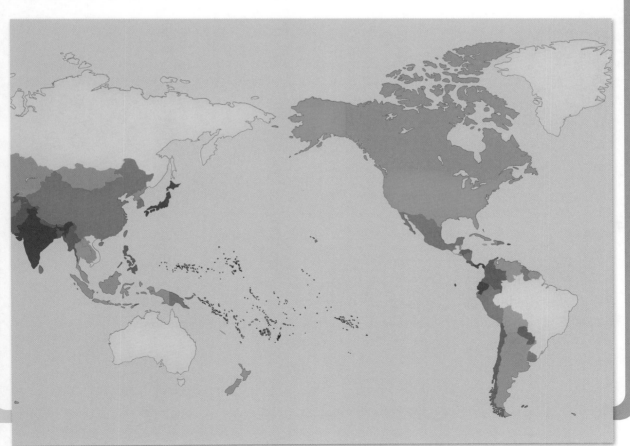

ISBN: 978-017023-077-3

Revising acronyms and country codes

Think about continuity and change: how the ideas and actions of people in the past have had impact.

Acronyms (initialisms) use the first letter or first parts of words to make an abbreviation. Usually a writer will present the full name when he or she uses it first in a story and after that use the acronym. For example, 'The Ku Klux Klan wanted to adopt a bit of highway to clean up but some people were horrified that a so-called racist group would be allowed to, despite the KKK saying it would not wear its white robes and hoods while cleaning.'

Practice 1

> **Skill: Critical thinking**
> - Think logically. For example, in an effort to be PC and not discriminate against non-Christians, some people use the term B.C.E.
> - I, O, W often mean International, Organisation, World.

Supply the missing information in the following.

AL	_____ League
ANZUS	_____ New Zealand United States Security Treaty
APEC	Asia Pacific _____ Cooperation
ASEAN	Association of Southeast Asian _____
AWOL	_____ without leave
B.C.E.	Before the Common _____
CIS	Commonwealth of _____ States
EEZ	_____ Economic Zone
EU	European _____
FAO	Food and _____ Organisation
GATT	General Agreement on Tariffs and _____
GDP	Gross _____ Product
GNP	Gross _____ Product
IAEA	International Atomic _____ Agency
ILO	International _____ Organisation
IOC	International Olympic _____
IRA	Irish _____ Army
NASA	National Aeronautics and _____ Administration
NATO	North _____ Treaty Organisation
NGO	Non _____ organisation
OECD	Organisation of Economic _____ and Development
OPEC	Organisation of the Petroleum _____ Countries

ISBN: 978-0170230-77-3

UNESCO	United Nations Educational, Scientific and _____ Organisation
UNICEF	United Nations _____ Fund
UNHCR	Office of the United Nations High Commissioner for _____
WHO	World _____ Organisation
WTO	World _____ Organisation
WWF	World _____ Fund
ODA	_____ Development Assistance
USSR	_____ of Soviet Socialist Republics (used before Dec 1991)

Practice 2

Below are some codes that many international sporting organisations, including the Olympics, use. See how many you can crack.

> **Skill: Code-cracking**
> - As the codes need to be clear rather than secret, logic will help you.
> - If there are letters that don't seem to fit a country, think of what else they might stand for; for example, R could be Republic, K could be Kingdom, F could be Federated.
> - Another language beside English may play a part; for example, the Spanish language is Espanol, and a country might have a French name. There is also one country here that has a double-barrelled name.

AUS _____	AUT _____
BIH _____	BRN _____
CHI _____	CHN _____
ESP _____	FRA _____
FSM _____	GBR _____
GRE _____	INA _____
IND _____	IRL _____
ISL _____	KSA _____
LBA _____	LBR _____
LIB _____	MAR _____
MAS _____	MDV _____
NED _____	NZL _____
PRK _____	RSA _____
SOL _____	SUI _____
SWZ _____	TGA _____
TUV _____	USA _____
VAN _____	ZIM _____

ISBN: 978-0170230-77-3

23 Understanding globalisation

Think about the economic world: how people seek economic growth through business and how economic decisions impact on people and countries.

Globalisation refers to movement - how culture, ideas, languages, people, technology, information, and economic activity, are increasingly moving around the world. You can buy McDonald's fast food in countries such as Qatar, Oman, Venezuela, Andorra, El Salvador; New Zealand in 2012 had 152 McDonald's. Very often globalisation is about economics - the global distribution of the production of goods and services, through reduction of barriers such as tariffs (taxes) to international trade. Some experts say globalisation has been around for a long time and some say it is a myth, but most say modern globalisation started in the 1980s. There is much dispute about whether globalisation is good or bad for the world.

Practice 1

The chart contains points that experts use to argue for or against globalisation. Colour the arguments for with one colour and the arguments against with another colour.

Skill: Sorting information
- This involves sorting the points into pros and cons. Your job is just to sort them, not decide if you think the arguments are right or wrong.
- For each point, ask if the person thinks it is a good thing or a bad thing; for example, 'more immigration including illegal immigration' suggests the person thinks it is a bad thing.

corporations look for cheap labour so they provide jobs in developing countries	
loss of jobs in developed countries	improves transportation of goods and people
increases investment in developing countries by developed countries	
increases free trade among countries	allows vital information to be shared
increases the chances of economic disruptions in one country affecting many countries	
reduces possibility of war between countries because they see the world as a global village	
more immigration including illegal immigration	more international travel and tourism
reduces diversity in the world	more international cultural influences, such as Hollywood
international groups like the World Trade Organisation get too powerful	
increase in the share of the world economy controlled by multinational corporations	
spreads the idea of materialistic lifestyles and consumption being the way to prosperity	
increases the risk of diseases being carried unintentionally between countries	increases the chances of wars between groups and countries as they vie for resources
increases knowledge and tolerance of different peoples	competition keeps prices down
some groups who lack resources won't be able to function within increased competition	

ISBN: 978-017023-077-3

increases the chance of environmental disasters as polluting corporations take advantage of weak environmental rules in developing countries	
increases the chance of violence when groups try to preserve their culture	
it could develop a new world political order	better access to products from different countries
increases the flow of communication	spreads ideas of democracy to developing countries
more sharing of information by the spreading of technology	increase in standards applied globally such as copyright laws

Practice 2

Study the images and do the activities beside them.

Skill: Describing a connection
- This asks you to think of the relationship between a key word and an image.
- Use what you worked with in Practice 1 to distinguish different themes of globalisation such as communication and economies.

Describe how you would alter this image to link it more closely to the idea of globalisation.

_____
_____
_____
_____
_____
_____

Describe how the image is linked to the idea of globalisation.

_____
_____
_____
_____
_____
_____

Describe how the image is linked to the idea of globalisation.

_____
_____
_____
_____
_____

ISBN: 978-0-17023-077-3

24 Recognising culture in action

Think about culture, identity and organisation: how cultural interaction impacts on cultures and societies.

Practice 1

Skill: Representing
- This asks you to think about how an image expresses or symbolises something.
- Refer back to the chart to make sure you have understood the meanings of the terms.

Study the chart. Then study the images and do the activities that accompany them.

Cultural interaction: relationships between or among different cultures

Cultural integration: people adopt cultural norms of the majority or host culture while keeping their own culture which allows differences to be peacefully accommodated

Cultural differences: specific differences such as Samoan lavalava and Indian sari

Cultural diversity: categories for cultural differences, such as food, building, art, literature, music, beliefs, values, traditions (Note: people often use cultural diversity to mean cultural differences)

Cultural assimilation: minorities reject or lose their own culture and adopt or are absorbed into the majority's culture

Cultural separation: individuals reject the dominant or host culture in favour of keeping their culture of origin

Cultural segregation: the state keeps cultures apart deliberately

Cultural borrowing: adoption of a specific element of one culture by another culture

Cultural diffusion: spread of cultural items such as technologies and religions

Culture shock: surprise, disorientation, and fear people can have when they meet a new culture

Cultural awareness: being sensitive to different cultures and understanding how their ways may be different to your own

Cultural hearth: place such as Nile Valley from which things like agriculture spread.

This man is suffering culture shock. Describe how he is feeling and why.

_____
_____
_____
_____

Explain how you could use this image to describe the meaning of cultural interaction to someone.

_____
_____
_____
_____

ISBN: 978-017023-077-3

Explain how this is a symbol of unfinished cultural assimilation.

Explain how climate change can threaten cultural diversity.

_____
_____
_____
_____

_____
_____
_____
_____

Practice 2

Write in the cultural terms that best match the following. Use 'c' as an abbreviation for 'cultural'.

Skill: Activating prior knowledge
- This is recalling what you learnt in Practice 1.
- Refer back to the chart if you are unsure; this will help reinforce the knowledge. Do this as often as you need to.

1 Inuit eat seal-meat; recently a man was jailed in New Zealand for attacking a seal. _____

2 Whites Only sign in South Africa under apartheid system of government. _____

3 Acceptance of adopted country's laws without losing your own birth culture. _____

4 Jews forced into Jewish ghettoes within European cities. _____

5 Sometimes given negative names such as cultural theft. _____

6 Cocoa cola products are found even in remote Himalayan villages. _____

7 Mecca is this for Islam as Muslims travelled from there to convert people. _____

8 New members of a society being indistinguishable from older members. _____

9 White means purity in Japanese culture, and funerals and mourning in China. _____

10 Muslims can experience this when they see Western women in short skirts. _____

11 British pop group The Spice Girls incorporated the haka into their stage act. _____

12 The UN says this is as necessary for humankind as biodiversity is for nature. _____

13 White rapper Eminem used hip hop in the movie 8 Mile. _____

14 Not when coach demands a player attend a match on the player's Sabbath. _____

15 New Zealand has freedom of religion. _____

16 Starbucks is found even in China's Forbidden City. _____

17 Music festival where different cultural groups sing. _____

18 Many cities around the world have a Chinatown. _____

19 Spread of companies such as McDonald's could lead to loss of this. _____

20 In one country a firm, short handshake is correct, in another a limp, long one is. _____

ISBN: 978-017023-077-3

Keeping up with the growth of sustainability

Think about the economic world: how management of resources impacts on environmental and social sustainability.

Practice 1

Study the following and after each describe why it is good for sustainability.

Skill: Integrating
- This involves connecting and combining information.
- Do this by combining information you know already (that sustainability means using resources wisely so they will be available for future generations) with what you read. For example, the bottle temple uses recycled material to produce something that is easy and cheap to clean, does not fade, does not pollute, is beautiful to look at and attracts tourists.
- It is therefore a sustainable solution that is good economically, socially and environmentally.

Buddhist monks in Thailand have used one and a half million recycled brown and green beer bottles to build a temple. The ability of the glass to let light shine through it and to hold thermal mass give a stained glass effect. Even washrooms and the crematorium are built of bottles. Mosaics around the temple are made from used bottle caps.

_____
_____

Now available are tiny containers of growing plants to wear as pendants or brooches. You can also get ones that attach to your bike.

_____
_____

A new wind turbine that can produce clean drinking water from the air can even work in the desert. Energy created from the turbine is used to power the heating of air, so driving out moisture. This steam is then condensed and collected.

_____
_____

The Solar Tulip is an energy-generating tower that produces electricity from sunlight and hot air. Mirrors trained on the flower-shaped tower heat air inside and as it expands it is forced through a turbine. Waste heat can be used for industrial and agricultural processes. As the Tulip is modular it can take additions.

_____
_____

The world's first vertical forest grows on the sides of 27-storey twin towers known as the Bosco Verticale in the Italian city of Milan. Trees were tested with wind turbines to find the hardiest varieties. Each apartment has a balcony planted with trees. The filtering and reuse of greywater produced by the apartments provides irrigation.

_____
_____

ISBN: 978-017023-077-3

After sales of the huge, gas-guzzling Hummers dropped, a firm designed a house using the strength and durability of Hummer shells. The Hummer house has a solar power system, soy-based insulation, grey water recycling and geothermal heating and cooling.

After the earthquake damaged Christchurch Cathedral a temporary cardboard cathedral was designed with cardboard tubes on an A-frame of timber beams and steel.

Practice 2

Read the following and put its sustainability attributes on the diagram.

Skill: Identifying attributes

- **Attributes** are features and qualities of something or someone.
- This asks you to identify attributes that are specifically about sustainability. For example, does the first sentence contain a specific point about sustainability or is it just setting the scene?
- Summarise each attribute in a few words only.

Meridian Energy with its alliance partners Antarctica New Zealand constructed the world's southernmost wind farm at Ross Island in Antarctica which was officially opened in January 2010 to help provide power to the two scientific bases of New Zealand's Scott Base and USA's McMurdo Station. It reduces the amount of fossil fuels consumed, reduces transport costs and the environmental risks associated with transporting diesel fuel to and around Antarctica. Vehicles at Antarctica pose risks to wildlife and vegetation and anything involving fuel there has to be carefully monitored such as minimising the handling and storage of fuel near sensitive areas like fresh water, vegetation and animal colonies, and using drip-trays and sorbant mats when refuelling. Maintainance of the turbines is not labour-intensive because just small teams of technicians are needed.

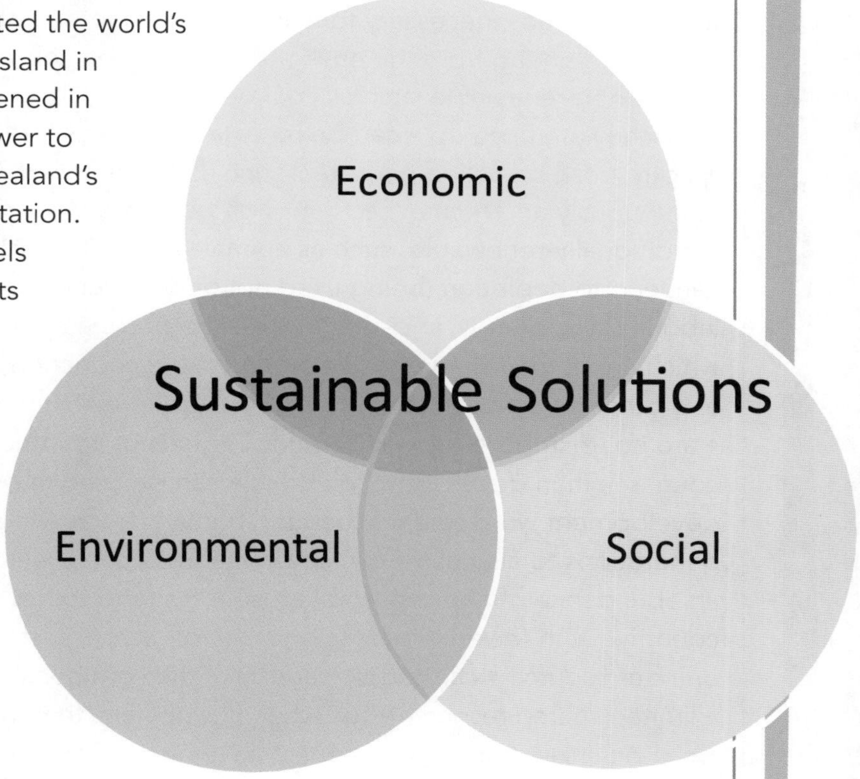

Economic
Sustainable Solutions
Environmental
Social

ISBN: 978-017023-077-3

26 Linking resources with sustainability

Think about the economic world: how the way people manage resources has impacts for environmental and social sustainability.

Practice 1

Use the data sheet to help you make a collage of terms and words to do with resources. Make sure you know their meanings before you use them.

Skill: Representing
- This means changing the form of information to show how critical elements are related; for example, instead of listing all New Zealand's resources you could use the term 'Resource-rich New Zealand'.
- To ensure clarity limit each term in the collage to single words or a few only words.
- Use different colours so terms are easily distinguishable.

Resources • are assets from which humans can draw to produce goods and services that meet needs (necessary for survival) and wants (desires) • can be natural or land resources coming from the environment • can be conserved and used sustainably • can be non-renewable such as coal because they form so slowly they can't be renewed once they are used up • can be renewable such as forests because they can form quickly • can be called perpetual such as air and wind, because they are available continuously and human consumption generally does not affect their quantity • can be conditionally-renewable, such as animals and soil, which means that overconsumption can lead to depletion (being used up) or destruction • can be human through the labour, skills, energy, and abilities used to produce goods and services • can be capital which are human-made goods or means of production such as machinery, buildings, and other infrastructure • have increasing demands on them from increasing population • are not distributed equally among regions or countries • are used more by developed countries than developing countries • can be used in conjunction with sustainable development which means meeting human needs while conserving for future generations to also use • can cause resource curse which is the idea that countries with an abundance of non-renewable resources tend to have less economic growth than countries with fewer resources because of factors such as corruption and concentration on one resource • can cause 'tragedy of the commons' where many individuals take from a limited shared resource even when it is obvious that this is not good in the long run • can be linked with ethical consumerism where buyers concern themselves with issues such as making sure the human rights of producers have been looked after • can be extracted from the environment such as New Zealand's resources of coal, gas, oil, gold, pounamu, salt, ironsand, petroleum, limestone, marble, volcanic rock such as basalt and hinuera stone, silver, platinum, copper, iron, molybdenum, titanium, antimony, chromium, lead-zinc, mercury, nickel, tin, tungsten, bentonite, brick clays, diatomite, dolomite, pumice, sulphur.

ISBN: 978-0-17023-077-3

Practice 2

Use the image to write a few sentences about the link between resources and sustainability.

Skill: Focussing
- Focussing (also spelt focusing) is a core thinking skill that involves selecting pieces of information and ignoring others. Here you need to focus on how resources are used.
- Go back to the data sheet and re-read the points about sustainability and renewable and non-renewable resources. This will help explain the image.

Biofuel mustard crop.

_____

_____

_____

_____

_____

_____

ISBN: 978-0170-23-077-3

Practising multi-choice and sentence answers

Think about the economic world: how people's management of resources impacts on sustainability.

Practice 1

Skill: Decision-making
- Remember that where all answers could be correct there will be one that is more correct.
- Make sure you know the meaning of the key word sustainability.
- Always refer back to the text before you make a final decision.

Read the following and circle the correct answers in the questions about it.

In a recent month of 2012, bad news on the issue of sustainability included the fact that about 500,000 tonnes of clothes are landfilled each year which is equivalent to the weight of the world's tallest building, the Burj Kalifa, and that many coffee growers in East Timor, where people do not have enough to eat, earn a pittance for their produce which sells in New Zealand for up to 140 times the money received by the growers. Good news included many innovations such as the new Pure Water Bottle which sterilises dirty water by eliminating 99.9 percent of bacteria and viruses. Using a 4 micron-sized water filter and wind-up ultra-violet light system does away with chlorine and iodine tablets and their unpleasant taste, and cuts sterilisation time from 30 to two minutes. The Enervate powertread mat takes energy created by the weight and speed of a car driving over it and converts it into electricity. Enervate estimates that on an industrial scale, the mat can generate 15 kilowatts an hour – enough power for 12 houses. The Copenhagen Wheel turns a normal bicycle into a hybrid-electric one by harnessing energy lost through braking and storing it in a compact battery on the back wheel to be recovered later by an electric motor. A solar firm has developed a solar cell to embed into windows to generate enough electricity during the day to give night lighting for the house. Another innovation is an electric motorcyle with a maximum speed of 112 km/h and a range of 100 kms. The Waldorf-Astoria New York, one of the city's most famous hotels, has introduced honeybees on its 20th floor and plans to harvest honey. The bees will also help pollinate new trees that are part of the city's plan to plant one million trees over the next decade. An experimental solar-powered plane landed in Morocco after a 20-hour flight from Madrid in the first transcontinental journey by a craft of its type. Although 12,000 solar cells were fitted across its wings, which have the same span as a Boeing 777, the plane weighs only as much as an average family car. The solar panels charge the batteries for night-flying. Morocco is building a huge solar energy farm as part of a project to lessen dependence on fossil fuels and produce 2000 megawatts of solar energy by 2020. A pile of refrigerators that were removed from Hackney in preparation for the London Olympics 2012 were turned into an outdoor movie theatre which played athlete-themed movies like Rocky, and aimed to raise awareness about the number of fridges going to landfills.

ISBN: 978-017023-077-3

1 A pittance is a
   a) low payment   **b)** reasonable payment   **c)** high payment.

2 The transcontinental flight was from
   a) Asia to Europe   **b)** Europe to Africa   **c)** Europe to North America.

3 Over half the 11 examples mentioned are mainly to do with
   a) speed   **b)** experiments   **c)** energy.

4 The best definition of a hybrid is a
   a) solar cell   **b)** mixture   **c)** harnessing.

5 The number of places mentioned by name is
   a) three   **b)** six   **c)** nine.

6 The project furthest from completion is most likely to be the
   a) solar energy farm   **b)** Olympics   **c)** tree plantings.

7 The highest item is most likely to be the
   a) Copenhagen Wheel   **b)** hotel honeybee farm   **c)** Burj Kalifa.

8 The number of recycling examples mentioned is
   a) one   **b)** two   **c)** three.

9 The wing-span of the solar-powered plane would best be described as
   a) immense   **b)** average   **c)** short.

10 A micron would be used to measure
   a) a kilowatt   **b)** a particle   **c)** ultra-violet light.

11 The coffee-growing issue is least concerned with
   a) social sustainability   **b)** environmental sustainability   **c)** economic sustainability.

12 To assess the Pure Water Bottle's sustainability it would be most useful to know
   a) the material it is made of   **b)** its size and shape   **c)** its inventor's nationality.

Practice 2

Skill: Information-gathering
- This involves bringing information to your consciousness.
- Start with the title – what does it suggest the graphs are about?
- Compare and contrast graphs if there is more than one.
- Note any qualifying words such as 'around' or 'about' which may be used to describe projected figures.

Study the graphs and write a few sentences about what information they provide.

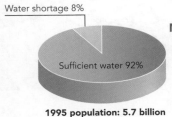

Water shortage 8%

Sufficient water 92%

1995 population: 5.7 billion

More of the population will suffer water shortages:

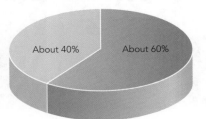

About 40%   About 60%

2050 population: 9.1 billion (projected)

_____

_____

_____

_____

ISBN: 978-0-17023-077-3

Making sense of headlines

Think about continuity and change: how events have causes and effects and how the ideas and actions of people in the past impact on people's lives.

A **headline** is a title of an online or offline newspaper story, and it will either encourage or discourage you to read what comes after it. An effective headline grabs your attention, sends you a message and promises to pay you back for the time you spend reading the story.

Practice 1

Underline the **dates** and **headlines** below. Study the form of each headline and use your observations to fill out the chart about headlines.

> **Skill: Observing**
> - This is an information-gathering skill that involves obtaining data through one or more methods; here you are asked to study several resources and make conclusions.
> - Think about what all or most of the resources have in common. For example, do any of them use the past tense?
> - If there is only one that is different to the others you can say 'mostly' or 'generally' to show this.

Location (where you find it in story)	
Voice (active eg. Dog saves man, passive eg. Man is saved by dog)	
Verbs (doing words)	
Adjectives (describing words)	
Punctuation	

ISBN: 978-017023-077-3

Sentences	
Tense (present eg. saves, past eg. saved)	
Capitals	
Use of a, an, and, the	
Emphasis	

Practice 2

Write headlines that could be used for stories about the following summaries.

Skill: Creative thinking
- This means being original and appropriate; you can be direct by simply stating or indirect by trying to arouse curiosity.
- Leave your own feelings out of it; for example, you may think Peter Jackson doesn't deserve the recognition but you need to record only that he got it.

1 Special step by Queen to mark Diamond Jubilee, Peter Jackson, Oscar-winning director of The Lord of The Rings and King Kong made Additional Member of the Order of New Zealand, June 4 2012. _____

2 Universal Declaration of Human Rights adopted by United Nations General Assembly, 10 December 1948, at Palais de Chaillot in Paris. _____
_____

3 Beginning of London Olympics, 28 July 2012, promised to be world's first sustainable Games, measuring carbon footprint, stadium most sustainable ever built, zero waste-to-landfill, food sustainably sourced. _____

4 Christchurch earthquake 22 February 2011, 12.51 pm., magnitude 6.3, depth 5 km., near Lyttelton, calving from Tasman Glacier, tsunami waves in Lake Tasman, landslides, deaths, injuries.
_____

5 Rugby World Cup win by NZ, Webb Ellis Cup, beat France in final 8-7 at Eden Park, Auckland, October 23 2011._____

6 Hurricane Katrina, 29 August 2005, much of city (which sits below sea level) was submerged, killed 1,836 in Louisiana and Mississippi. _____
_____

7 October 2011 world population reached 7 billion, increasing at rate of 78 million per year.
_____

8 29 April 2011, Prince William married Catherine Middleton. _____
_____

9 July 25, 1978, world's first successful test-tube baby was born in Great Britain.
_____

10 August 1 1987 Maori became an official language of New Zealand.
_____

ISBN: 978-017023-077-3

Appreciating cartoons

Think about culture, identity and organisation: how people pass on and sustain culture and heritage.

Not everyone has the same sort of humour but cartoons tend to have broad appeal because they are a graphic and clever comment on a current event or issue.

Practice 1

Study the cartoon and answer the questions about it.

Skill: Analysing
- Analysing is examining methodically and in detail. Here the task is easier because you have questions to guide you. If you put your answers together you would have an analysis.
- Always examine any extra information you are given. Here there is a caption which helps explain the cartoon.

THE **ABC** OF FLAGS — TREMAIN

A THE NEW ZEALAND FLAG — FLOWN AS A SYMBOL OF NATIONAL UNITY.

B TINO RANGATIRATANGA FLAG — FLOWN TO CONTRADICT **A**

C THE WHITE FLAG — WAVED BY THE KEY GOVERNMENT WHENEVER FACED WITH MAORI DEMANDS.

On Waitangi Day 2010 the national Maori flag flew for the first time over the Auckland Harbour Bridge. It also flew in Wellington - at Parliament, Premier House (official residence of the Prime Minister), the National War Memorial and a number of government departments. The decision in 2009 by the government to fly the Maori flag as well as the traditional NZ flag next Waitangi Day was controversial.

1 Who is the cartoonist and where is this name shown? _____

2 What is the title of the cartoon? _____

3 What does 'the abc' of something mean? _____
_____

4 How has the cartoonist linked this meaning to the flags? _____
_____

5 What colours appear in the flags and why? _____
_____

6 Which flag shows a relationship with another country and why? _____
_____

7 Which flag features a fern frond? _____

8 Which flag best shows a relationship to the Commonwealth? _____

9 What official position is 'Key' most likely to hold and why do you think that? _____
_____

ISBN: 978-017023-077-3

10 What is a white flag most commonly used for around the world? _____
_____

11 Which flag is best described at the traditional New Zealand flag? _____

12 Which flag is used by Maori to show Maori chieftainship? _____

13 How might flag B be seen to contradict flag A? _____

14 How does the cartoon suggest the decision to fly flag B was controversial? _____
_____

15 Which group does the cartoon suggest is the most likely one wanting flag B to be flown?
_____

16 In what way can a flag be a symbol of national unity? _____
_____

17 Did this cartoon appear on Waitangi Day? Give a reason for your answer. _____
_____

18 Give a second reason for your answer. _____
_____

19 How has the cartoonist repeated the idea of ABC in the layout of the cartoon? _____
_____

20 Does the cartoon suggest what the attitude of the cartoonist might be to the issue, and why do you think that? _____

Practice 2

Study the cartoon below and formulate 10 questions that would help people analyse it.

Skill: Formulating questions
- Formulating means expressing in a concise and precise way – short and to-the-point.
- Make sure questions are not ambiguous – able to be taken two or more ways.
- Use your prior knowledge; for example, Dickens (1812-70) wrote books such as *Oliver Twist* and *Great Expectations* which are still famous, not only in England but around the world.
- Consider things such as visual devices like relative sizes, and how culture and heritage is preserved.

2012 cartoon from Allan Hawkey

1 _____
2 _____
3 _____
4 _____
5 _____
6 _____
7 _____
8 _____
9 _____
10 _____

ISBN: 978-0170-23-077-3

Think about identity, culture and organisation: how groups make decisions that impact on communities.

Practice 1

Put 'less likely or 'more likely' after each item in the table to show how today's Kiwi youth differ from previous generations. Then study the graph and complete the sentences about it.

Skill: Activating prior knowledge
- This involves using what you have learnt in the past, such as how previous societies worked and how to analyse a graph.
- Think logically, such as seeing a connection between statements 4, 5, and 10 in the table.

1	To have two parents who live together.	_____
2	To have more access to personal technology.	_____
3	To have step or blended family relationships.	_____
4	To be more ethnically diverse.	_____
5	To have grown up with greater exposure to different cultures.	_____
6	To have fixed gender roles.	_____
7	To be less educated.	_____
8	To be married.	_____
9	To be parents.	_____
10	To identify as European.	_____

1 The source of the graph is _____

2 Young people are defined as _____

3 The x axis shows _____

4 The y axis shows _____

5 Projected means _____

6 The number of young people is expected to _____

7 At the 1996 census young people made up just over _____ of the total population.

8 The proportion of youth population has fallen since _____

9 Projections show the proportion of young people will decline until at least _____

10 Projections assume medium levels of fertility and _____

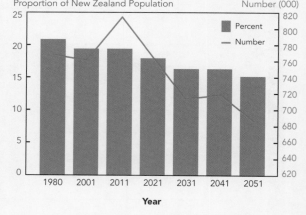

Proportion and Projected Number of New Zealand Population Aged 12-25 Years

Source: Statistics NZ

ISBN: 978-017023-077-3

Practice 2

Use your logic and knowledge to help you answer the following.

Skill: Activating prior knowledge
- This involves using what you have learnt in the past, such as youth issues and comprehension exercises.
- Think logically. For example Question 2 is obviously about sound, so think of what rhymes with 'sport'.

1 Sometime in the 4th century BC the famous Greek philosopher Plato said, 'What is happening to our young people? They disrespect their elders, they disobey their parents. They ignore the law. They riot in the streets inflamed with wild notions. Their morals are decaying. What is to become of them?' What does his comment and the date of the comment suggest? _____
   _____

2 Finish this often-quoted rhyme, 'A kid in sport stays out of _____'

3 Is it legal for parents to allow their under-age child to drink at home or any other private place?
   _____

4 The four pillars of a young person's life are said to be family, school, community and _____

5 Is it illegal for a person under the drinking age to buy alcohol at the request of a Police officer?
   _____

6 Rainbow Youth in New Zealand is for youth who identify as _____

7 What is meant by the comment 'Love the skin you're in'?_____

8 Some issues for youth are drugs, alcohol, suicide, bullying, violence, obesity, eating disorders, sexually-transmitted diseases, road deaths. Are these issues specific to youth? _____

9 What are the police doing if they caution you? _____

10 What term is used for someone who is not yet old enough to legally drink? _____

11 Drinking large amounts of alcohol all at once is known as what? _____

12 The Ministry of Youth Affairs aims to improve the ability of all young people to reach their full potential. What does that mean? _____

13 The Ministry aims to offer solutions for young people who are 'at risk'. What is an 'at risk' person? _____

14 If you are under the drinking age what is the only way you can enter a bar or nightclub? _____
   _____

Questions 15 to 20 refer to the following. Recently Government said it would invest $62 million over four years to address youth mental health issues, including New Zealand's high youth suicide rate. Components included putting more nurses and specially trained youth-workers into low decile secondary schools and expand the Positive Behaviour School-Wide programme into all secondary schools. Government agencies were to overhaul the mental health-related resources they produced to ensure they were youth-friendly and technologically up-to-date. That would include investigation of technology, such as Facebook and online pop-ups, to reach young people and provision of E-therapy specifically tailored for young people.

15 What is E-therapy most likely to be? _____

16 What is meant by a low decile school? _____

17 What criteria was Government using to evaluate mental health-related resources produced by its agencies? _____

18 Which general youth issues is the money to address? _____

19 Which specific youth problem issue is mentioned? _____

20 What is an online pop-up? _____

ISBN: 978-017023-077-3

Think about identity, culture, and organisation, and continuity and change: how systems of government affect people's lives, how the ideas and actions of people in the past have had impact on people's lives.

Amongst the sources of New Zealand's constitution are various statutes such as the Electoral Act and the Bill of Rights Act, and, say many experts, the Treaty of Waitangi. Local governments have to take the Treaty into account, as do various developments such as health promotion. No other country has a Treaty of Waitangi yet many people from other countries study it as an example of past, present and future cultural interaction.

Practice 1

Examine the profiles of the 10 people who had key roles in bringing the Treaty of Waitangi into existence. From the names in the bottom box, select who you think the people are and write their names with their profiles.

Skill: Identifying

- This asks you to establish and indicate who someone is. Read the profiles carefully.
- Work from basics first; for example, how many Maori names are supplied? Is there a French-sounding name?

Head of English Church Mission Society in New Zealand. With son Edward had one night to translate English draft of Treaty into Maori. Difficult task; eg. used 'kawanatanga' (governance) to translate 'sovereignty' and 'tino rangatiratanga (full authority) over 'taonga' (treasures) for 'undisturbed possession' of all properties. Had to explain Treaty to chiefs at Waitangi.
French bishop sympathetic to Maori concerns and culture. At Treaty hearing asked for pledge to protect Catholic faith; pledge sometimes referred to as unwritten fourth article of Treaty, said to protect and recognise major western religions and Maori custom.
British citizen and businessman in New Zealand, official position of Consul of United States. Reported important political developments related to New Zealand to Washington D.C. Said to be one of several who created final English draft of Treaty handed over for translation into Maori.
Nga Puhi chief, early friend of Pakeha. Said British intervention necessary for peace and order, governor should be father, judge and peacemaker but Maori customs to be preserved and land never taken. Helped win argument for Treaty and was among first to sign.
Landed at Bay of Islands 30 January to read proclamation of his appointment as Lieutenant-Governor, arranged meeting of chiefs at house of British Resident on 5 February. On 6 Feb said to each signing chief - 'He iwi tahi tatou' (We are all one people) – only te reo he knew. Became Governor at end of 1840 when New Zealand became British colony.
Church Mission printer at Bay of Islands. Printed Treaty in Maori. Present at Treaty signing, later published eyewitness account of event drawn from notes he had made.
Nga Puhi chief, first to sign Treaty as wanted Governor to stay and be like father to Maori to stop French and rum sellers taking over. Later opposed British and ordered cutting down of flagpole at British settlement of Kororareka (later called Russell).

ISBN: 978-017023-077-3

Sailed from Bay of Islands on HMS Herald to get Treaty signatures; told to complete negotiations in North Island areas that had not been covered and in South Island. Edward Williams acted as interpreter for trip.

British Resident based at Waitangi. Had no troops or police or legal power to make arrests so known as Man-o-War without guns. Helped draft Treaty. His home and grounds was location for Treaty explanations, debates and signing; now called Treaty House.

Of Ngati Toa and Ngati Raukawa, migrated from Kawhia to Kapiti Island area to escape conflict with Waikato tribes. Strong leader. One of 13 women to sign Treaty, at time when women in Britain did not have vote.

James Busby, Thomas Bunbury, James Clendon, William Colenso, Hone Heke, William Hobson, Tamati Waka Nene, Jean Baptiste Pompallier, Rangi Topeora, Henry Williams

Practice 2

See how many of the following questions about the Treaty you can answer without research.

Skill: Recalling
- Given the significance of the Treaty it is worthwhile you having at least a basic understanding of it. Think about what you have learnt in the past.
- Use logic and critical thinking to help retrieve relevant data; re-reading Practice 1 might help.

1 Date signed (day, month, year)? _____

2 Where Waitangi is? _____

3 British monarch at the time? _____

4 Reason Hobson acted on monarch's behalf? _____

5 One reason for Treaty? _____

6 Another reason? _____

7 And another reason? _____

8 Meaning of rangatira? _____

9 Meaning of rangatiratanga? _____

10 Number of articles in the Treaty? _____

11 Languages that versions of the Treaty were written in? _____

12 Most chiefs who signed, signed the version in which language? _____

13 Reason Treaty went around country for others to sign? _____

14 After the signing, under British law New Zealand became a Crown what? _____

15 Maori are indigenous people; meaning? _____

16 At this time, Maori often called Aborigines. Meaning? _____

17 Reason British maybe surprised Maori women signed Treaty? _____

_____

18 Reason Government confiscated some Maori land after 1860s Wars? _____

_____

19 Two places you can view the Treaty? _____

20 Today Treaty is called New Zealand's what document? _____

ISBN: 978-0-17023-077-3

32

Committing to a process

Think about continuity and change: how the Treaty of Waitangi is responded to differently by people in different times and places.

Commitment is an aspect of knowledge and self-control that involves the decision to use personal energy towards understanding. As the Waitangi Tribunal may affect you directly or indirectly, it is worth investing time to understand it.

Practice 1

Read the material below about the Waitangi Tribunal process. Highlight information you did not know. Then underline 10 key words or phrases you would use in a PowerPoint presentation about how the Waitangi Tribunal process works.

Skill: Commitment
- Tackle the task by doing exactly as the instructions say – read (this means close reading), highlight (this means honestly) and underline (this means thoughtfully).
- Use what you already know; for example, tribunal = person or group who have authority to judge or sort out a claim or dispute, Crown = government of New Zealand, breach = breaking a law or promise, process = series of actions bringing about a result.

The Waitangi Tribunal was set up in 1975 to be a permanent commission of inquiry on claims brought by Maori. Claims are complaints that the Crown has breached the Treaty by action, inaction, law, or policy and that Maori have suffered harmful effects as a result. Claims may be made only against legislation or the Crown, not against individuals. Claims can be historical such as claims for compensation over confiscated land or contemporary such as saying a current Government policy, action, or inaction is in breach of Treaty principles. The Tribunal has the right to refuse to inquire into a claim. It has up to 20 members appointed by the Governor-General on the recommendation of the Minister of Maori Affairs; about half are Maori and half are Pakeha. Its chairperson is either a judge or a retired judge of the High Court or the chief judge of the Maori Land Court and its deputy chairperson is a judge of the Maori Land Court. The Tribunal generally prefers to hear claims at the areas to which they relate and at any given time will be working on a number of enquiries. Once a claim is submitted, it is checked to see if it is appropriate, registered and given a Wai number. Tribunal hearings are open to the public and times are published in local and regional newspapers. Two types of evidence are usually presented. Technical evidence comes from researchers into archival material; tangata whenua (or customary) evidence comes from claimants and may include graphics such as maps and written and oral submissions such as waiata or korero. The Tribunal can conduct its own research to try to find the truth of a matter but can not stop something from happening or make something happen; nor can it make a party to its proceedings pay costs. The Crown has an opportunity to challenge evidence by cross-examining witnesses and submitting evidence of its own. The Tribunal produces a report of its findings for the claimants and the Crown. In most cases, while Government must consider the recommendations it does not have to act on them.

ISBN: 978-017023-077-3

Practice 2

Read the following. Highlight the Maori terms and make sure you know their meanings. Then answer the questions that follow.

Wai 262, lodged in 1991, was about issues such as who controls Maori traditional knowledge, artistic and cultural works such as haka and waiata, and the environment that created Maori culture. It was also about the place in society of Maori cultural values such as the obligation of iwi and hapu to act as kaitiaki towards taonga such as traditional knowledge, artistic and cultural works, important places, and flora and fauna that are significant to iwi or hapu identity. In 2011, the Waitangi Tribunal released its very long report on the Wai 262 claim. Its recommendations included the Crown establish a system that allows anyone to object to derogatory or offensive public uses of taonga works, taonga-derived works and related knowledge. The system should also allow kaitiaki to object to commercial uses or proposed commercial use of taonga works and related knowledge that do not have their consent. It recommended greater weight be given to kaitiaki interests when decisions are made about genetically modified organisms and a system be set up to allow kaitiaki priorities for the environment to be integrated into decision-making. It recommended ways to sustain Te Reo, Matauranga Maori and rongoa, such as ensuring that traditional healing plants survive and that tohunga can access them.

1 Why is the Waitangi Tribunal unique to New Zealand? _____

_____

2 What is a difference between the Tribunal and a court of law? _____

_____

_____

3 What does Wai 262 stand for? _____

4 Suggest a reason for the long gap between lodging of the claim and the report on it. _____

_____

5 Lego used the words tohunga and tapu on children's plastic toys, Philip Morris marketed a brand of cigarettes called Maori Mix in Israel and singer Moana Maniapoto could not use her own name on a CD because a German company had taken out an international trademark on the Maori name. Explain how such uses could be said to be derogatory or offensive. _____

_____

_____

6 Could you have attended any of the hearings about Wai 262? _____

7 Does it seem the Tribunal generally supported the original claim or not? _____

8 Is the Crown legally bound to act on all the recommendations? _____

9 Explain why or why not you could one day lodge a complaint to the Tribunal. _____

_____

10 State your opinion: Should a pop group be allowed to do the haka on stage as part of their act?

_____

ISBN: 978-017023-077-3

33

Thinking about conflict

Think about continuity and change: how events have causes and effects, how the ides and actions of people in the past have had impact on people's lives.

Practice 1

Study the types of conflict in the chart and highlight each one as you understand how it occurs. Then give your attitudes to the examples of conflict that follow.

Skill: Expressing attitudes
- Attitudes are your beliefs and principles, and ways of thinking and feeling, that govern your actions. Expressing them helps to communicate who you are.
- You can express an attitude about something by stating feelings, how it makes you act, or your belief and knowledge about it; for example, '*I am pleased Kiwis are recycling and I will continue to encourage them to do so as I believe it is good for sustainable growth.*'

Personal conflict: Features such as culture, religion, gender, values, interest, hopes and ethnicity can cause conflict with people who are different to you.

Racial conflict: Ethnicity gives people a sense of identity and belonging, and when that is threatened by things like racial taunts and abuse, people can react violently.

Political conflict: This can arise when government takes away human rights from people, or when a group wants to break away.

Ideological conflict: This is about people fighting for ideas and ideals and of how things should be, rather than fighting for personal gain.

Religious conflict: Conflict can arise when a religious group is attacked or penalised, or if the group tries to spread its belief or force it on others.

International conflict: When all efforts to resolve conflict between or among nations fail, war can break out.

Class conflict: Examples are landlords versus peasants, lower or middle classes versus the upper class, the low place of the Untouchables in India's caste system.

Group conflict: Inter-group conflict is between different groups such as a young generation and an old one; intra-group conflict is between people from the same group.

Economic conflict: This can arise when resources such as land, water, jobs, and housing are scarce or not distributed equitably, or when employers clash with workers.

Judicial conflict: This is when people hire lawyers to sort out conflict.

1 Strike action by employees _____

_____

2 Racist comments from one soccer player to another _____

_____

3 Social classes _____

_____

4 Religious conflict _____

_____

5 Intra-group conflict _____

_____

ISBN: 978-017023-077-3

6 Ideological conflict _____

_____

7 Family feuds _____

_____

8 Gang warfare _____

_____

9 Road rage _____

_____

10 Hollywood divorces _____

_____

11 Present world conflicts _____

_____

12 Future world conflicts _____

_____

Practice 2

Skill: Self-knowledge
- There are no right or wrong answers here; you just need to be honest.
- Knowing yourself is power knowledge and a step towards success.

Experts have proposed many models for conflict resolution. The following are points on which most agree. Use one colour to highlight ones you already employ in conflict resolution, and another colour for ones you can learn.

Recognise that conflicts continue to fester when ignored.	Use active listening skills to ensure you hear and understand other positions and perceptions.	
Avoid disrespectful words and actions.	Recognise that conflicts trigger strong emotions.	
Be calm, patient, alert and non-defensive.	Control emotions and behaviour; don't threaten, frighten or punish.	Focus on the now.
Know that conflict can be draining and so you need to consider whether the issue is worthy of your time and energy.	Know that you must agree on the problems to solve before you will find a mutually acceptable solution.	
Focus on the issues and leave personalities out of the discussion.	See the conflict from the other person's point of view.	Identify issues clearly.
Accept that conflicts are an opportunity for growth and trust-building.	Be open to conflict-resolution and solving a problem through discussion and negotiation.	
Understand that we respond to conflicts based on our perceptions of the situation which may not be an accurate view.	Use 'I' statements to explain how you feel and what you would like to happen, rather than 'You' statements which can cause a defensive reaction.	
Make your first priority maintaining and strengthening the relationship, rather than 'winning' or 'being right'.	Be ready to move on without holding resentment or anger.	
Try to see the conflict and its impact objectively: Is it disrupting team work? Slowing down decision-making?	Know when to let something go. If you can't resolve the conflict, you can choose to disengage and move on.	
Brainstorm possible solutions, and be open to all ideas.	Aim for a win-win solution rather than a win-lose solution.	

ISBN: 978-017023-077-3

Think about continuity and change: how events have causes and effects.

Practice 1

Read the following and highlight types of warfare with one colour, causes of war with another colour and results of war with a third colour.

War is the ultimate conflict because enemies aim to defeat and often destroy each other with military technology. Generally, the more sophisticated the weapons the more damage - bows and arrows do not cause the same carnage as a nuclear war which could make humans extinct. Death and disruption to Maori tribes in New Zealand increased when Maori added European guns to traditional weapons. Conventional warfare does not use nuclear, biological or chemical weapons. Nuclear warfare has so far been limited to the US dropping an atomic bomb on Hiroshima and another on Nagasaki in 1945. Biological warfare uses material such as bacteria, viruses and fungi. Examples are poisoning wells with a fungus or infected animals, shooting infected arrows, throwing clay pots full of venomous snakes on to enemy ships, lobbing plague-ridden bodies over castle or city walls, giving smallpox-infected blankets as gifts, infecting animals and feed with anthrax. Chemical warfare agents include chlorine gas, mustard gas, defoliants such as Agent Orange. A civil war is between groups from the same country such as government forces and rebels. Guerilla warfare is where small groups use ambushes, sabotage, and raids against the enemy and leave immediately. A cold war is conflict between nations that instead of direct military action uses tactics such as spying, and economic and political actions. Trench warfare is where opposing forces dig trenches in which to shelter from enemy fire and from which to launch attacks across No-Man's Land. Warfare is also named after the surface on which it is fought, such as jungle, urban, naval, desert. Wars can have strange names, such as the War of Jenkins' ear between Great Britain and Spain. Wars erupt for many reasons. The Crusades were originally about European Christians fighting 'Holy Wars' against the Saracens (Moslems) to get access to sites such as Jerusalem. The War over Water was a series of confrontations between Israel and its Arab neighbours over water sources in the Jordan River Basin and Golan Heights. The war in Iraq was partly about conflicting ideologies and partly about the oil resources which Saddam Hussein controlled. Contributing to the Vietnam War was the US fear that communism could expand throughout Southeast Asia. World War II showed up many examples of nationalism such as Japanese kamikaze pilots and Hitler's desire to expand Germany's territory. The on-going Kashmir conflict is a territorial dispute between India and Pakistan over Kashmir. US and UK forces invaded Afghanistan in 2001 to find al-Qaeda members, to destroy the organisation, and to

ISBN: 978-017023-077-3

remove the Taliban, an extremist Muslim group who harboured al-Qaeda. While war leads to improvements of technology, it can also cause death, injury and psychological damage to people, including civilians, and soldiers might carry out atrocities against civilians. Diseases and infection among troops may spread to civilians. Ruined crops and trade blockades lead to hunger and starvation, loss of homes leads to refugees. Economies suffer through money being spent on war, lost production, destruction of infrastructure and resources, destruction of crops and farm animals, damage to the environment. Society is further disrupted by black-market selling or war-materials selling, and some people supporting war and some opposing it. After a war there can be continuing danger with buried landmines, unexploded shells, and chemical agents. Resentment arrives when losers have to pay war reparations or give up land to winners.

Practice 2

Study the images and then write a comment about each, explaining how it is linked to war.

Skill: Retrieval
- This is about accessing previously encoded information. For example, you may know specific details you can add to your responses such as the Ancient Greek mythology about Helen of Troy.
- It will help if you refer back to Practice 1.

1 _____

2 _____

3 _____

4 _____

5 _____

6 _____

7 _____

8 _____

ISBN: 978-017023-077-3

Index and Skills summary

ISBN: 978-017023-077-3